FIVE COMMITMENTS OF REPENTANCE WORKBOOK

DEUTERONOMIC CYCLE

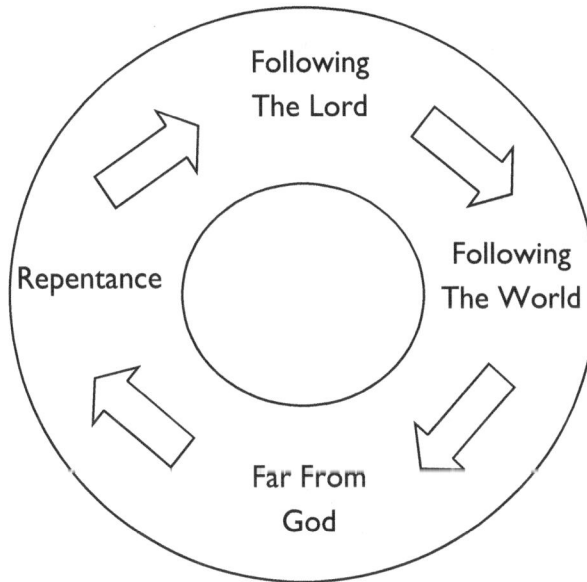

Following The Lord → **Following The World** → **Far From God** → **Repentance** → (back to Following The Lord)

WHERE DO YOU THINK WE ARE AS A NATION?

By David Lange

Five Commitments of Repentance
By David E. Lange

Copyright © 2009 David E. Lange

Unless otherwise indicated, Scripture quotations are taken from the HOLY BIBLE: NEW INTERNATIONAL VERSION®. © 1973, 1978, 1984 International Bible Society. Used by permission of Zondervan. All rights reserved.

Scripture quotations marked NLT are taken from the *Holy Bible,* New Living Translation, copyright 1996, 2004. Used by permission of Tyndale House Publishers, Inc., Wheaton, Illinois 60189. All rights reserved.

Graphic Artist: Jessica Dodson
Cover Picture by Peggy Dodson

Published by Lange Publishing, Pacific, MO
Library of Congress Control Number: 2009902949
ISBN 978-0-9824070-1-1
ISBN 0-9824070-1-7
Printed in the United States of America

This book is dedicated to . . .

Christy. She is my wonderful, supportive, and beautiful wife. Without the support of her and my three awesome kids, Jeremiah, Bethany, and Sofia, this work would not have been possible.

Dad and Mom. I cherish the godly parents that I have been blessed with.

Mission Community Church. I also want to acknowledge and thank our church family for putting up with me during this process.

Debra. My very supportive sister, her family, Jon Marc, Nathan, Micah, Natalie, and their church family, Katy Park Baptist Church.

Linda Jones. My favorite aunt, who was also the first editor of this work.

Of course the greatest honor and glory goes to Jesus Christ, my Lord and Savior!

CONTENTS

INTRODUCTION   I

THE FIVE COMMITMENTS   4

LESSON ONE   **6**

WHERE WE ARE AS A COUNTRY   18

COMMITMENT ONE   24

LESSON TWO   **41**

COMMITMENT TWO   48

LESSON THREE   **60**

COMMITMENT THREE   67

LESSON FOUR   **81**

COMMITMENT FOUR   87

LESSON FIVE   **98**

COMMITMENT FIVE   107

REFLECTION   123

DEDICATION   133

LESSON SIX   **144**

SNARES OF SATAN BIBLE STUDY   151

FOR PASTORS AND TEACHERS   **157**

ANSWERS TO THE LESSONS   158

INTRODUCTION

Where do you think we are as a country? Would you say that we are following the Lord or that we are far from God? Every day our country moves closer and closer to pushing God out. Prayer has been removed from our school systems, the Ten Commandments have been taken off of our courthouses, and there are lawsuits against the Bible.

William J. Federer, a leading historian who writes about the destruction of our nation, points out just how far we have fallen. In his book *What Every American Needs to Know about the Qur'an* he reveals just how close we are to losing the freedoms that we hold so dear. I would encourage you to read through it and see the destruction that is right around the corner. What can we do? How can we stop the destruction of our country? Is it happening because Christians are not politically active enough? Do we need more zeal in our fight to defend God's Word?

I am all for people voting and being active in politics as long as they keep a Christlike servant attitude, but I do not believe we need more political activism. God does not need anyone to defend His name or to protect His people. I repeat, God does not need anyone to defend His name or to protect His people. What he needs is for His people to be holy, as He has commanded us.

There is a cycle throughout the Old Testament that is called the Deuteronomic Cycle. The nation of Israel would continually go through this cycle. They would be close to God and experience his blessings, and then they would gradually begin to follow the ways of the world and eventually end up at the bottom of the cycle, far from God. If the nation refused to repent, they would go into exile and slavery. Their freedoms to worship God would be attacked and they would be forced to serve another. Is this happening in our country?

America is going through this cycle. We began this country based upon the laws of God, and because of this we have been blessed tremendously! As the nations before us, we have gradually turned away from God to follow the ways of this world. We are committing spiritual adultery with the world around us. If we cannot see that we are in desperate times and that desperate measures of repentance are needed, we will go into slavery.

Many Christian leaders can see that our country is in need of revival, and we quote this verse often, hoping that if we repent, God will heal our land.

> **2 Chronicles 7:14:** *If my people, who are called by my name, will humble themselves and pray and seek my face and turn from their wicked ways, then will I hear from heaven and will forgive their sin and will heal their land.*

One of the things that we must do before God will heal our land is to turn from our wicked ways. Do we have wicked ways? Isn't the moral decline of our country dependent upon the ungodly actions of our government? After all, we did not vote for abortion and we did not ask them to remove the Ten Commandments. So it is their fault, right? Wrong. The leadership that we have in our country is dependent upon the obedience of God's people. If God's people decide to turn away from Him and follow the ways of this world, then God will allow us to have leaders from the world. We will be overtaken and driven into slavery just as the cycle reveals.

I want to challenge you to take a very serious look into your own life to see if you have allowed wicked ways into your life. Let's not blame others but let's allow God's Word to reveal to us our wicked ways.

This book is a result of what the Lord has been doing in my life. He is revealing to me, a pastor, how I have turned away from Him to follow the ways of the world. It is a wake-up call to all of us to return to our first love and pray that God will heal our land. I have broken this call into five commitments.

Don't just read through the commitments and think, "Well I'm doing those things." Read through this book and see if your standards are God's standards. Just to give you a little taste of how far we have turned away from God, I will give you some insight into where we are headed. Did you know that Christian bookstores now sell movies that have cursing in them and they take the Lord's name in vain?

Are we now more enlightened than our ancestors of the faith who would have abstained from such evil? Are we more mature or are we more deceived? Take the journey with me. Repent, and then encourage other churches and Christians to get on board in order for God to heal our land. Are you a five-commitment Christian? Is your church a five-commitment church?

THE 5 COMMITMENTS OF REPENTANCE

ABSTAIN FROM IMMORALITY

I commit that I will abstain from whatever presents immorality as acceptable. I will be aware of Satan's tricks and I will stand up for God's morals. I will get rid of the moral filth, based upon God's Word, that I have allowed into my life and I will be holy to the Lord. (Deuteronomy 7:26; 8:10–14; 1 John 5:19; Ephesians 2:2; 5:3–7; 2 John 2:7–11; James 1:21; Exodus 20:7; Colossians 3:8; 1 Peter 2:11; 1 John 1:8, 9)

MAKE PRAYER AND GOD'S WORD A PRIORITY

I will make prayer and God's Word a priority in my life and my family's life. I will discipline myself to my quiet times, and I will make opportunities where we read and pray together as a couple or family. (Matthew 4:4; Psalm 1:1; 119:11; Deuteronomy 6:4–9; 32:45–47; 1 Thessalonians 5:17; Hebrews 4:12)

HONOR THE SABBATH

I commit that I will no longer miss church for work, for things of this world, for entertainment, for laziness, or for selfish reasons. I will no longer honor the changing of the blue law, but I will honor God's Law. I realize that I reap what I sow. I am ready to stand up for Jesus and His Word and to call the church back to Him. (Isaiah 56:2; 58:13,14; 1 John 2:15–17; James 4:4; Leviticus 19:1–3; Exodus 20: 8–11; 31:13–17; Acts 20:7; Revelation 1:10)

BRING IN THE TITHES AND OFFERINGS

I will not rob God. I will bring in the whole tithe and offering. I will do this cheerfully because I love and trust God for all of my blessings. I also realize that our nation is under a curse because of our unfaithfulness in this area. (2 Corinthians 8:19; 9:6–7; Malachi 3:6–18; Matthew 23:23)

MAKE DISCIPLES

I will be a disciple maker. I realize the moral decay of the church and our country, and I am willing to call people back to God. I understand that I will be persecuted, but I am willing to stand up for Jesus and make disciples. (Mark 8:34, 35; Matthew 5:10; 28:18–20; John 15:4–16; Luke 16:9; 2 Timothy 1:7; 3:12; Galatians 2:20; 1 John 2:6; Amos 6:1–7; Ezekiel 3:18–20; Acts 20:26; 26:18; 2 Corinthians 5:17–20)

LESSON ONE: ABSTAIN FROM IMMORALITY

WHERE WE ARE AS A COUNTRY

We began this country based upon the laws of _____ (1), and because of this we have been blessed tremendously! As the nations before us, we have gradually turned away from God to follow the ways of this world.

DEUTERONOMIC CYCLE

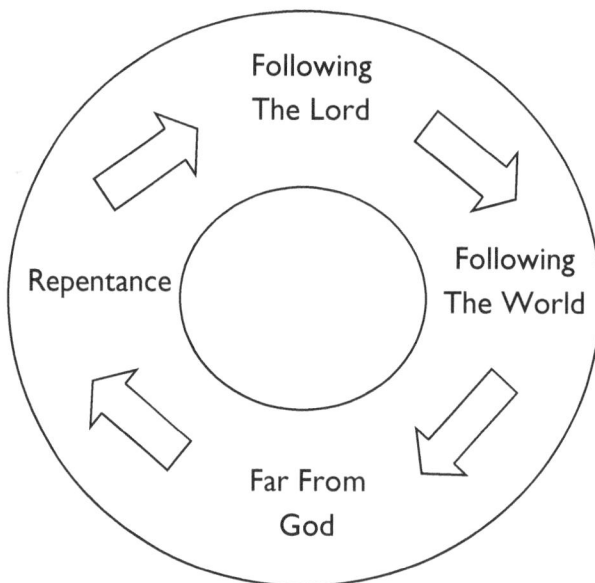

Following The Lord

Following The World

Repentance

Far From God

Deuteronomy 4:5–8: See, I have taught you decrees and laws as the LORD my God commanded me, so that you may follow them in the land you are entering to take possession of it. Observe them_____ (2), for this will show your wisdom and understanding to the nations, who will hear about all these decrees and say, "Surely this great nation is a wise and understanding people." What other nation is so great as to have their gods near them the way the LORD our God is near us whenever we pray to him? And what other nation is so great as to have such righteous decrees and laws as this body of laws I am setting before you today?

DO THE MEDIA AND THE WORLD PERCEIVE CHRISTIANS TODAY AS WISE AND UNDERSTANDING?

I Kings 9:6–7: But if you or your sons turn away from me and do not observe the commands and decrees I have given you and go off to serve other gods and worship them, then I will cut off Israel from the land I have given them and will reject this temple I have consecrated for my Name. Israel will then become a byword and an object of _____ (3) among all peoples.

DO THE MEDIA AND THE WORLD RIDICULE CHRISTIANS AND LOOK DOWN UPON THEM?

A picture of the American church—

Deuteronomy 8:10–14: When you have eaten and are satisfied, praise the LORD your God for the good land he has given you. Be careful that you do not forget the LORD your God, failing to observe his commands, his laws and his decrees that I am giving you this day. Otherwise, when you eat and are satisfied, when you build fine houses and settle down, and when your herds and flocks grow large and your silver and gold increase and all you have is multiplied, then your heart will become_____ (4) and you will forget the LORD your God, who brought you out of Egypt, out of the land of slavery.

WHAT HAPPENED? HOW HAVE WE BECOME PROUD?

We have trusted in the wealth and not the _____
_____ (5). Once we became secure and comfortable, we
gradually began to follow the ways of the world.

> ***Deuteronomy 11:16–21:*** *Be careful, or you will be*
> *_____ (6) to turn away and worship other gods*
> *and bow down to them. Then the LORD'S anger will burn*
> *against you, and he will shut the heavens so that it will not rain*
> *and the ground will yield no produce, and you will soon perish*
> *from the good land the LORD is giving you.*

We have been enticed to turn away from God. The 5 commitments
address 5 specific ways he entices us.

OBEDIENCE EQUALS BLESSINGS AND DISOBEDIENCE EQUALS CURSES

> ***Deuteronomy 11:26–28:*** *See, I am setting before you today*
> *a blessing and a curse—the blessing if you _____ (7)*
> *the commands of the LORD your God that I am giving you*
> *today; the _____ (8) if you disobey the commands of*
> *the LORD your God and turn from the way that I command you*
> *today by following other gods, which you have not known.*

CAN YOU SEE THE PERSECUTION OF CHRISTIANS BUILDING?

Some of the curses we are experiencing:

_____ (9) removed from our schools

Ten Commandments removed from our courthouses

Legalized _____ (10)

The _____ (11) law changed

THE GOOD NEWS: GOD CAN HEAL OUR LAND, IF WE REPENT

> *2 Chronicles 7:14:* *If my people, who are called by my name, will humble themselves and pray and seek my face and turn from _____ (12) wicked ways, then will I hear from heaven and will forgive their sin and will heal their land.*

I want to challenge you to take a very serious look into your own life to see if you have allowed wicked ways into your life.

Did you know that _____ (13) bookstores now sell movies that have cursing in them and they take the Lord's name in vain?

THE 5 COMMITMENTS OF REPENTANCE

ABSTAIN FROM IMMORALITY

MAKE PRAYER AND GOD'S WORD A PRIORITY

HONOR THE SABBATH

BRING IN THE TITHES AND OFFERINGS

MAKE DISCIPLES

FOR GOD TO HEAL OUR LAND, WE MUST TURN BACK TO HIM

Humble ourselves. (Admit our sin and need for Him)

Pray. (Ask for forgiveness)

Seek His face. (Search the Scriptures, Relationship)

Turn from our wicked ways. (Repent)

COMMITMENT I ABSTAIN FROM IMMORALITY

**Abstain: to refrain deliberately and often with an effort of
_____ (14) from an action or practice
(*Webster's Dictionary*)**

THE PROGRESSION OF EVIL IN OUR COUNTRY

When television began, shows were more wholesome and
_____ (15) oriented.

One of the greatest ways to teach is through stories. Jesus taught through the telling of stories.

In an article in the American Family Association Journal the January 2009 issue on page 4 states, "The Parents Television Council found that profanity during primetime broadcast television has not only increased since 1998, but that harsher profanity has quickly risen in prominence." It goes on to state, "Not only are harsher profanities like the f-word and the s-word airing during hours when children are likely to be in the viewing audience, but they are occurring with greater frequency." Their results show that, "when an expletive is introduced on television, usage of the word becomes commonplace in fairly short order." Have you noticed how many Christians are using curse words? Have you noticed that there are "Christian" movies that have cursing in them and the taking of the Lord's name in vain?

When television first began, if Satan had presented to us the garbage that is on nightly, no one would have watched, but since he introduced it slowly, we have accepted more and more until we are where we are today.

One of Satan's big attacks is to get people to accept
_____ (16) as normal or moral.

We are so engrossed in the things of this world (movies, music, magazines, television) and listening to its teachings that we are slowly

_____ (17) what we are being taught.

Christian parents all across our country are scratching their heads and wondering why their children are acting in such immoral ways: having sex before marriage, getting pregnant, cursing, the lack of respect, the laziness, viewing homosexuality as normal, their lack of commitment to church, and on and on.

WHY IS SATAN WINNING?

We spend a few hours a week in church, and then the rest of the week we are taught by Satan through the movies, music, television, and things that we read. God has specifically warned us to stay away from the snares of our world; yet we have not heeded the warning. We are _____ (18) after the things of this world and we have forgotten to heed the laws of God. In this recurring Deuteronomic cycle we are beginning to experience the curses for our disobedience.

WHOSE STANDARD ARE WE TO FOLLOW? (NC-17, R, PG-13, PG, G)

Christian bookstores now sell movies with cursing and the taking of the Lord's name in vain in them. Certain "Christian" Web sites will review movies for us and even tell us of the immoralities in them and then tell us why they give the movie so many stars. How many stars would the Lord give a movie that takes His name in vain? _____ (19)

OUR FIGHT WITH SATAN

> *I John 5:19:* We know that we are children of God, and that the whole world is under the _____ (20) of the evil one.

> *Ephesians 2:1–2:* As for you, you were dead in your transgressions and sins, in which you used to live when you

followed the ways of this world and of the ruler of the kingdom of the air, the spirit who is now at work in those who are disobedient.

Who is it that is writing the movies, music, and other materials that are influencing us to disobey God?

There is an illustration told of a father who wanted to teach his children about the subtleties of sin. His children were begging him to allow them to watch a movie with only a little sin in it. After speaking with them about the dangers of such an endeavor, he decides to use an illustration to teach them. He carefully prepares some homemade brownies for them and then calls them in to feast on the sweet-smelling treats. He announces to his children, "I have taken great care to prepare these brownies for you using only the best ingredients, but I do need to tell you before you eat, that there is just a little bit of dog poop in them."

Therefore, our _____ (21), likes, or interests do not dictate what is moral.

GOD'S WARNINGS

> *Isaiah 5:20: Woe to those who call evil good and good evil, who put darkness for light and light for darkness.*

Are we not calling evil good when we _____ (22) movies, music, books, etc. that by God's nature He cannot watch?

> *I Peter 2:11: Dear friends, I urge you, as aliens and strangers in the world, to abstain from sinful desires, which _____ (23) against your soul.*

> *I Corinthians 6:18: _____ (24) from sexual immorality.*

Does this passage mean only that we are not to participate in sexual immorality, but we can watch or even own movies, music, and shows that depict it as moral?

GODLY PRINCIPLES

> *1 Corinthians 3:16: Don't you know that you yourselves are God's temple and that God's Spirit lives in you?*

PRINCIPLE: IF WE WOULD NOT SHOW IT, READ IT, OR LISTEN TO IT IN CHURCH, THEN IT SHOULD NOT BE ALLOWED IN OUR _____ (25). GUARD YOUR HEARTS.

> *2 John 1:7–11: Many deceivers, who do not acknowledge Jesus Christ as coming in the flesh, have gone out into the world. Any such person is the deceiver and the antichrist. Watch out that you do not lose what you have worked for, but that you may be rewarded fully. Anyone who runs ahead and does not continue in the teaching of Christ does not have God; whoever continues in the teaching has both the Father and the Son. If anyone comes to you and does not bring this teaching, do not take him into your house or welcome him. Anyone who welcomes him _____ (26) in his wicked work.*

The context of this passage is that many deceivers have gone out to lead people astray. In their day, it was traveling preachers, but in our day we allow teachings into our home that do not bring the teachings of Christ through the TV, radios, books, magazines, etc.

PRINCIPLE: WHEN WE BRING THINGS (MOVIES, MAGAZINES, MUSIC, ETC.) INTO OUR HOMES THAT DO NOT BRING THE TEACHINGS OF CHRIST, WE ARE _____ (27) IN THEIR WICKED WORK.

I Peter 1:14–15: As obedient children, do not conform to the evil desires you had when you lived in ignorance. But just as he who called you is holy, so be holy in _____ (28) you do.

PRINCIPLE: HOLINESS IN THE BIBLE MEANS SEPARATION FROM ALL THAT IS COMMON OR UNCLEAN. IN RESPECT TO GOD, HOLINESS MEANS THAT HE IS SEPARATE FROM ALL THAT IS UNCLEAN AND EVIL (*Basic Theology: A Popular Systematic Guide to Understanding Biblical Truth*)

God cannot be around our worldly movie, music, and book collections. Why then do we have it? How are we being _____ (29) by participating and supporting things that are evil and will not be in heaven?

WHY ALL OF THE TEMPTATIONS?

Deuteronomy 13:1–4: If a prophet, or one who foretells by dreams, appears among you and announces to you a miraculous sign or wonder, and if the sign or wonder of which he has spoken takes place, and he says, "Let us follow other gods" (gods you have not known) "and let us worship them," you must not listen to the words of that prophet or dreamer. The LORD your God is _____ (30) you to find out whether you love him with all your heart and with all your soul. It is the LORD your God you must follow, and him you must revere. Keep his commands and obey him; serve him and hold fast to him.

God does not want _____ (31). He desires to be worshiped by those that have a choice to worship Him.

OUR PROBLEM

We are all sinners, all of us has turned away (Romans 3). If we do not allow the _____ _____ (32) to enable and help us to be holy, we will turn away and be destroyed like the nations before us as Romans 3:20 points out.

THE SOLUTION: JESUS

> *Romans 3:22–26: This _____ (33) from God comes through faith in Jesus Christ to all who believe. There is no difference, for all have sinned and fall short of the glory of God, and are justified freely by his grace through the redemption that came by Christ Jesus. God presented him as a sacrifice of atonement, through faith in his blood. He did this to demonstrate his justice, because in his forbearance he had left the sins committed beforehand unpunished—he did it to demonstrate his justice at the present time, so as to be just and the one who justifies those who have faith in Jesus.*

THE MISUNDERSTANDING OF OUR DAY

Jesus did not die on the cross and save us from our sins in order for us to continue to live in them. He died on the cross to set us free from our sinful ways and desires.

> *Titus 2:11–12: For the grace of God that brings salvation has appeared to all men. It teaches us to say "No" to ungodliness and worldly passions, and to live self-controlled, upright and _____ (34) lives in this present age.*

Many times we twist the grace of God and we use it for a license for immorality. Jude speaks about this misunderstanding as well.

> *Romans 8:3–4: For what the law was powerless to do in that it was weakened by the sinful nature, God did by sending his own Son in the likeness of sinful man to be a sin offering. And so he condemned sin in sinful man, in order that the righteous _____ (35) of the law might be fully met in us, who do not live according to the sinful nature but*

15

according to the Spirit.

The questions then become: Would Jesus own this movie? Would Jesus go and support this movie? Would he listen to the same radio station that I do?

> **2 Corinthians 6:14–18:** *Do not be yoked together with unbelievers. For what do righteousness and wickedness have in common? Or what fellowship can light have with darkness? What harmony is there between Christ and Belial? What does a believer have in common with an unbeliever? What agreement is there between the temple of God and idols? For we are the temple of the living God. As God has said: "I will live with them and walk among them, and I will be their God, and they will be my people." "Therefore come out from them and be separate, says the Lord. Touch no _____ (36) thing, and I will receive you." "I will be a Father to you, and you will be my sons and daughters, says the Lord Almighty."*

To be yoked with an unbeliever is to listen to their advice and teachings. You might say, "Well I agree that taking His name in vain is a sin, but it is all right for me to own or watch movies that take His name in vain." Why would it be all right? Jesus would not own or watch such a movie, so why is it all right for us?

WAR, SELF-DENIAL, AND SUFFERING

> **1 Peter 2:11:** *Dear friends, I urge you, as aliens and strangers in the world, to _____ (37) from sinful desires, which war against your soul.*

> **Galatians 5:16–21:** *So I say, live by the Spirit, and you will not gratify the desires of the sinful nature. For the sinful nature desires what is contrary to the Spirit, and the Spirit what is contrary to the sinful nature. They are in _____ (38) with each other, so that you do not do what you want. But*

if you are led by the Spirit, you are not under law. The acts of the sinful nature are obvious: sexual immorality, impurity and debauchery; idolatry and witchcraft; hatred, discord, jealousy, fits of rage, selfish ambition, dissensions, factions and envy; drunkenness, orgies, and the like. I warn you, as I did before, that those who live like this will not inherit the kingdom of God.

I John 2:6: *Whoever claims to live in him _____ (39) walk as Jesus did.*

ABSTAIN FROM IMMORALITY

I commit that I will abstain from whatever presents immorality as acceptable. I will be aware of Satan's tricks and I will stand up for God's morals. I will get rid of the moral filth, based upon God's Word, that I have allowed into my life and I will be holy to the Lord. (Deuteronomy 7:26; 8:10–14; I John 5:19; Ephesians 2:2; 5:3–7; 2 John 2:7–11; James 1:21; Exodus 20:7; Colossians 3:8; I Peter 2:11; I John 1:8, 9)

BEFORE LESSON 2 READ THROUGH:

INTRODUCTION	I
WHERE WE ARE AS A COUNTRY	18
COMMITMENT ONE	24

WHERE WE ARE AS A COUNTRY

DEUTERONOMIC CYCLE

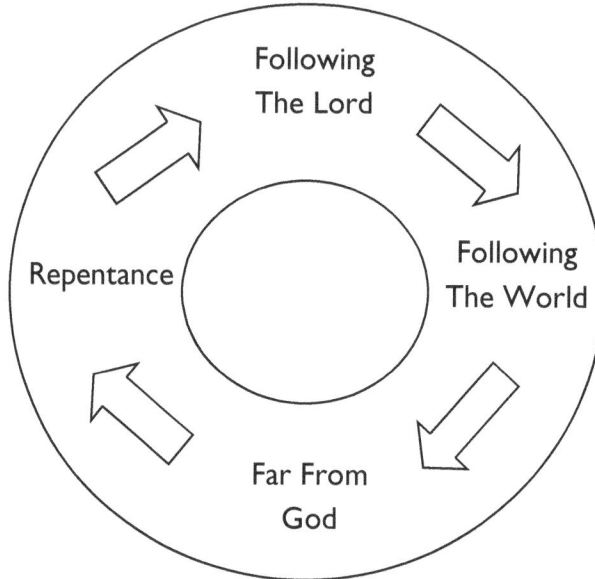

Following The Lord

Following The World

Far From God

Repentance

The Deuteronomic cycle is a recurring cycle in the Old Testament. From the graphic, you can see the trend of following the Lord and then slowly being enticed to turn away from the Lord to follow the world. At the bottom of the cycle when a nation is far from God, they begin to experience his judgments or curses for their disobedience. Most Christians believe that America is far from God and we can see the judgments coming, but what can we do? How can we get back to following the Lord? When our country was founded upon biblical principles, we were blessed because of the promises of our unchanging God. We have experienced tremendous blessings for establishing our laws based upon His Word. When a nation is following the ways of God, they are considered wise and understanding, but when a nation turns away from following His laws, they will become a byword and an object of scorn. Some believe that the judgments we are experiencing are because the world is becoming more corrupt. It is my contention that it is not the world becoming more corrupt but it is the church that needs to repent. God does not need His people to speak up for Him and defend His name; He needs His people to be holy. This book is written to present five specific areas in which we need to repent. Let's look at some of the principles set out for us in this Deuteronomic Cycle.

> **Deuteronomy 4:1–2:** *Hear now, O Israel, the decrees and laws I am about to teach you. Follow them so that you may live and may go in and take possession of the land that the LORD, the God of your fathers, is giving you. Do not add to what I command you and do not subtract from it, but keep the commands of the LORD your God that I give you.*

It is very important for God's people not to add or subtract from God's laws. Christians should be active in the political process, but I don't believe that our country's moral decay is a result of us not being active enough. **God does not need us to defend His name. He does not need us to keep the economy strong or to keep abortion illegal. What He needs is for His people to be holy in order for us to display His glory to the world.** When we are being His holy people, then His hands of protection do not allow such judgments. He will keep our economy strong and abortion illegal. If we turn away from His ways, we will be cursed. From the Old Testament we see the cycle of disobedience and we see God's hands of protection leaving His people who forget His laws and follow the ways of the world. We see this progression in America.

> **Deuteronomy 4:5–8:** *See, I have taught you decrees and laws as the LORD my God commanded me, so that you may follow them in the land you are entering to take possession of it. Observe them carefully, for this will show your wisdom and understanding to the nations, who will hear about all these*

decrees and say, "Surely this great nation is a wise and understanding people." What other nation is so great as to have their gods near them the way the LORD our God is near us whenever we pray to him? And what other nation is so great as to have such righteous decrees and laws as this body of laws I am setting before you today?

As verse six points out, we must follow the ways of God carefully. If we are following the ways of God carefully, then we will be considered wise and understanding to the nations around us.

DO THE MEDIA AND THE WORLD PERCEIVE CHRISTIANS TODAY AS WISE AND UNDERSTANDING?

When a nation turns away from following the ways of God, they will become a byword and an object of ridicule. Christians are seen as bigots, hypocrites, and weak-minded individuals who need a crutch to make it through life. We are not seen as wise and understanding.

> *I Kings 9:6–7:* But if you or your sons turn away from me and do not observe the commands and decrees I have given you and go off to serve other gods and worship them, then I will cut off Israel from the land I have given them and will reject this temple I have consecrated for my Name. Israel will then become a byword and an object of ridicule among all peoples.

DO THE MEDIA AND THE WORLD RIDICULE CHRISTIANS AND LOOK DOWN UPON THEM?

Since the media of today portrays Christians as a byword and an object of ridicule, then we must conclude that we are not following His ways carefully. We must take responsibility and look closely at our character and see if we are displaying Christlike qualities.

The Deuteronomic cycle presents a picture of what nations do when they turn away from God. When they become greatly blessed by God, they become proud and feel as though they deserve the blessings. They trust in their own hands and the leaders around them instead of trusting in the God who blessed them.

A picture of the American church—

> *Deuteronomy 8:10–14:* *When you have eaten and are satisfied, praise the LORD your God for the good land he has given you. Be careful that you do not forget the LORD your God, failing to observe his commands, his laws and his decrees that I am giving you this day. Otherwise, when you eat and are satisfied, when you build fine houses and settle down, and when your herds and flocks grow large and your silver and gold increase and all you have is multiplied, then your heart will become proud and you will forget the LORD your God, who brought you out of Egypt, out of the land of slavery.*

WHAT HAPPENED? HOW HAVE WE BECOME PROUD?

We have acted like the nations before us. We have built our fine houses and watched our economy soar. We have trusted in the wealth and not the wealth giver. Once we became secure and comfortable, we gradually began to follow the ways of the world.

> *Deuteronomy 11:16–21:* *Be careful, or you will be enticed to turn away and worship other gods and bow down to them. Then the LORD'S anger will burn against you, and he will shut the heavens so that it will not rain and the ground will yield no produce, and you will soon perish from the good land the LORD is giving you.*

To entice is to attract artfully or cleverly. Satan desires to arouse our sinful desires and entice us to follow him. It is exactly what he has been doing since he was kicked out of Heaven. We have been enticed to turn away from God. The 5 commitments address 5 specific ways he entices us.

21

OBEDIENCE EQUALS BLESSINGS AND DISOBEDIENCE EQUALS CURSES

> *Deuteronomy 11:26–28: See, I am setting before you today a blessing and a curse—the blessing if you obey the commands of the LORD your God that I am giving you today; the curse if you disobey the commands of the LORD your God and turn from the way that I command you today by following other gods, which you have not known.*

CAN YOU SEE THE PERSECUTION OF CHRISTIANS BUILDING?

With the hate speech laws on the rise and the attempt to legalize same sex marriage, we are on the verge of seeing the Bible labeled as hate speech. If our country comes to this, the Scriptures will most likely be outlawed and we will have to be like the Christians in other countries, hiding our Bibles and having secret meetings. Will we repent before we go further into slavery?

Some of the curses we are experiencing:

Prayer removed from our schools

Ten Commandments removed from our courthouses

Legalized abortion

The blue law changed

THE GOOD NEWS: GOD CAN HEAL OUR LAND, IF WE REPENT

> *2 Chronicles 7:14: If my people, who are called by my name, will humble themselves and pray and seek my face and turn from their wicked ways, then will I hear from heaven and will forgive their sin and will heal their land.*

Many people are using this verse to call the church back to God, but are we really processing what the verse says? It is not other people who need to turn from their wicked ways. It is me—I need to turn from my wicked ways. Many Christians of today feel secure in their morality, but we are not judging our morality against the right standard. The standard with which we are to judge our morality upon is God's Word.

FOR GOD TO HEAL OUR LAND, WE MUST TURN BACK TO HIM

<u>Humble</u> ourselves. (Admit our sin and need for Him)

<u>Pray.</u> (Ask for forgiveness)

<u>Seek</u> His face. (Search the Scriptures, Relationship)

<u>Turn</u> from our wicked ways. (Repent)

COMMITMENT 1

ABSTAIN FROM IMMORALITY

THE FIRST COMMITMENT:
ABSTAIN FROM IMMORALITY

I commit that I will abstain from whatever presents immorality as acceptable. I will be aware of Satan's tricks and I will stand up for God's morals. I will get rid of the moral filth, based upon God's Word, that I have allowed into my life and I will be holy to the Lord. (Deuteronomy 7:26; 8:10–14; 1 John 5:19; Ephesians 2:2; 5:3–7; 2 John 2:7–11; James 1:21; Exodus 20:7; Colossians 3:8; 1 Peter 2:11; 1 John 1:8, 9)

Abstain: to refrain deliberately and often with an effort of self-denial from an action or practice (*Webster's Dictionary*)

THE PROGRESSION OF EVIL IN OUR COUNTRY

Satan has gradually desensitized us to sin. He has gradually gotten us (the church) to accept things that our ancestors would never have accepted—from the movies we watch to the magazines we read and the music we listen to.

When television began, shows were more wholesome and family oriented. What shows do you remember watching twenty years ago? Did they have the cursing, nudity, and taking of the Lord's name in vain that is on nightly? How sensitive are you to sin? Does it bother you to see nudity, hear cursing, or hear the Lord's name taken in vain? Have you been desensitized?

One of the greatest ways to teach is through stories. Jesus taught through the telling of stories. Through them we learn what to do and what not to do. Satan knows this truth and he tells stories as well. He tells them through movies, music, books, magazines, and other such avenues. His goals are opposite of the Lord's. His goal is to get us to disobey the commands of God. In an article in the *American Family Association Journal* the January 2009 issue on page 4 states, "The Parents Television Council found that profanity during primetime broadcast television has not only increased since 1998, but that harsher profanity has quickly risen in prominence." It goes on to state, "Not only are harsher profanities like the f-word and the s-word airing during hours when children are likely to be in the viewing audience, but they are occurring with greater frequency." Their results show that, "when an expletive is introduced on television, usage of the word becomes commonplace in fairly short order." Have you noticed how many Christians are using curse words? Have you noticed that there are "Christian" movies that have cursing in them and the taking of the Lord's name in vain?

Statistically, Satan is winning the battle of discipleship in the church. We are becoming more and more immoral. George Barna has presented this progression. From the divorce rate to our views on homosexuality, he presents the moral decline of the church. (Resources: barna.org and codebluerally.com)

George Barna wrote a book called *The Frog in the Kettle* several years ago. The book depicts the illustration of a frog being slowly boiled to death versus a frog thrown into a pot of boiling water. If you take a frog and place it in a pot of lukewarm water and slowly turn the heat up, it will remain in the water until fully cooked; however, if you take a frog and put it in a pot of boiling water, it will immediately jump out. Satan is doing the same thing with us—slowly desensitizing us to sin. **When television first began, if Satan had presented to us the garbage that is on nightly, no one would have watched, but since he introduced it slowly, we have accepted more and more until we are where we are today.**

One of Satan's big attacks is to get people to accept homosexuality as normal or moral. If we were to take a survey on this topic, you would see the decline in the generations. The older generations would be confident that homosexuality is a sin against God. Their children would be mixed in their views, and their grandchildren would be struggling to call it sin. Why?

We are so engrossed in the things of this world (movies, music, magazines, television) and listening to its teachings that we are slowly believing what we are being taught. Do you see the number of shows that present homosexuality as moral? Can you hear the news media and other sources crying out to us to accept this as normal and not to view it as sin?

We have been slowly desensitized to sin so that many Christians no longer hear the cursing; they no longer hear the Lord's name taken in vain. As a result, many Christians curse and take the Lord's name in vain. Saying, "Oh my _____" is taking His holy name in vain and breaking the Second Commandment. Have you noticed how many teenagers text the Lord's name in vain? OM____ is taking His name in vain. In the Old Testament the Jews would not even say His name for fear they would be using it in vain. Today, many Christians misuse it and have no concern for their actions. Why? Because we have been so desensitized to hearing it that we now use it ourselves. I have been amazed at how many Christians come up to me and ask me if I have seen a certain movie and then in my research I find that it has several immoralities in it. When I ask them if they remember hearing any of these immoralities they usually respond, "No, I didn't even know that was in there." There is a "Christian" movie (one that has no immoralities presented as acceptable) called Time Changer that depicts a man who has been transported to the future and he is amazed at the moral decay of society. In fact, he enters into a movie theater to watch a movie and then he begins to scream in the theater, "Stop the movie, and turn it off." He then runs out of the theater utterly appalled at what he has just seen and heard. Perhaps we should be so sensitive to sin.

Christian parents all across our country are scratching their heads and wondering why their children are acting in such immoral ways: having sex before marriage, getting pregnant, cursing, the lack of respect, the laziness, viewing homosexuality as normal, their lack of commitment to church, and on and on.

WHY IS SATAN WINNING?

We spend a few hours a week in church, and then the rest of the week we are taught by Satan through the movies, music, television, and things that we read. God has specifically warned us to stay away from the snares of our world; yet we have not heeded the warning. We are running after the things of this world and we have forgotten to heed the laws of God. In this recurring Deuteronomic cycle we are beginning to experience the curses for our disobedience. Eventually, we will be in slavery as the cycle displays. The world will turn on us and seek to destroy us. Can you see it coming?

WHOSE STANDARD ARE WE TO FOLLOW? (NC-17, R, PG-13, PG, G)

Everybody has a different standard as to what they will accept. In the world's standard even G-rated movies can take the Lord's name in vain. When *Gone with the Wind* was released, the powers that be had to change the standard to get that famous curse word in. Some accept cursing; some accept nudity; some accept violence; some accept sexual immorality. What standard should we be going by? When *Gone with the Wind* came out, many Christians boycotted the movie. Yet today many Christians display it proudly in their homes.

Christian bookstores now sell movies with cursing and the taking of the Lord's name in vain in them. Certain "Christian" Web sites will review movies for us and even tell us of the immoralities in them and then tell us why they give the movie so many stars. How many stars would the Lord give a movie that takes His name in vain? Zero! God cannot be around sin and He would not own anything that would go against His laws. Why then do we handle and touch immoral things?

OUR FIGHT WITH SATAN

Many have forgotten that there are two powers in the world and we are not one of them. We are either under the power of Satan or we are under the power of God. Unbelievers are under the power of Satan and they are being used by him to complete his work.

> **I John 5:19:** *We know that we are children of God, and that the whole world is under the control of the evil one.*

> **Ephesians 2:1–2:** *As for you, you were dead in your transgressions and sins, in which you used to live when you followed the ways of this world and of the ruler of the kingdom of the air, the spirit who is now at work in those who are disobedient.*

The Scriptures teach us that Satan is at work, controlling individuals to accomplish his ends. What are his desires? To get us to gradually turn away from God. How does he do it? He slowly entices and ensnares us to disobedience until we are where we are today, desensitized to sin. We need to get back to the struggle and stop giving in to our desires to be entertained.

> **Ephesians 6:11–12:** *Put on the full armor of God so that you can take your stand against the devil's schemes. For our struggle is not against flesh and blood, but against the rulers, against the authorities, against the powers of this dark world and against the spiritual forces of evil in the heavenly realms.*

Who is it that is writing the movies, music, and other materials that are influencing us to disobey God?

Are there exceptions to immorality? What if the movie is funny? What if the movie has a hero? What if the movie has a little truth? There is an illustration told of a father who wanted to teach his children about the subtleties of sin. His children were begging him to allow them to watch a movie with only a little sin in it. After speaking with them about the dangers of such an endeavor, he decides to use an illustration to teach them. He carefully prepares some homemade brownies for them and then calls them in to feast on the sweet-smelling treats. He announces to his children, "I have taken great care to prepare these brownies for you using only the best ingredients, but I do need to tell you before you eat, that there is just a little bit of dog poop in them." Is it really just a little bit of sin? Will that sin not grow if we plant it? Will it not increase the more we accept? Watch out for the yeast of evil!

I used to love going to see James Bond movies. It was so exciting to see the hero defeat the forces of evil. The action, the excitement, the thrill, the fun—but the more the Lord began to reveal to me, the more I became aware of the snares of Satan. Even though the movie depicts some good, it is also filled with subtle and blatant immoralities. For example, the movie depicts to young men that for them to be cool and the hero, they need to be playboys and commit sexual immorality. This was presented as moral and acceptable. Most of the movies that Satan is presenting to us use this subtle teaching element. Put in some good in order for them to accept the immoralities. With this discipleship method Satan is winning. His media presentations are far more appealing than Sunday school or Bible study. There is more action and excitement and it appeals to our sinful desires. We want to be the cool, proud hero. We want to be accepted and liked. We are failing to teach self-denial from such immoralities. Parents, this is one area that we are failing in—discipleship. We take our children to church for just a few hours a week and then we allow them to be taught by Satan the rest of the week.

I am the pastor of a church and I would be considered very conservative in my media choices, but I have also been ensnared and enticed, as well. I like to watch the nine o'clock news, and several years ago right after the news a show would come on called *Friends*. They would begin each show with a funny skit, and since I love to laugh, I was slowly drawn into the show. Gradually, I would watch a little more and accept a little more until the Lord finally spoke to me, "What are you watching? What are you supporting? Why is it okay for you but not your kids to watch this?" It was at this point that I began to repent and reevaluate my media choices based upon God's Word and not my opinions and desires. Today in church services, many Christian leaders quote movies and show clips that the Lord would never endorse. They watch shows that the Lord is appalled at, they listen to music that teaches immorality, and they are not calling the church to abstain from immorality. We must awaken to our sin and repent, if God is going to heal our land.

Satan tries to get us to accept our sinful desires as normal or moral. If it is funny or if we enjoy it then surely it must be okay to participate in. Right?

Currently, if someone is drawn toward homosexuality, Satan seeks to twist the truth and make it seem normal. God must have created me this way. What if the desire is to murder or molest children? Did God create that desire?

Therefore, our desires, likes, or interests do not dictate what is moral. If left on our own, our standards would be all over the place and they would gradually shift toward accepting more immorality. All are sinners. No one seeks God.

GOD'S WARNINGS

> *Isaiah 5:20:* Woe to those who call evil good and good evil,
> who put darkness for light and light for darkness.

Are we not calling evil good when we support movies, music, books, etc. that by God's nature He cannot watch? He cannot be around sin. He is holy.

> *I Peter 2:11:* Dear friends, I urge you, as aliens and strangers
> in the world, to abstain from sinful desires, which war against

your soul.

I Corinthians 6:18: *Flee from sexual immorality.*

Does this passage mean only that we are not to participate in sexual immorality, but we can watch or even own movies, music, and shows that depict it as moral? Would Jesus watch or own such things? Look at the evidence of the church since we have begun to accept watching, listening, and reading such immoralities. Our children resemble what they are allowing into their lives. Satan is discipling them. When will we call the church to abstain?

Philippians 4:8: *Finally, brothers, whatever is true, whatever is noble, whatever is right, whatever is pure, whatever is lovely, whatever is admirable—if anything is excellent or praiseworthy—think about such things.*

How do we know what is true, noble, pure, lovely, or admirable? Should we go by our desires or likes, or are we to go by God's Word or His morality?

2 Corinthians 11:3: *But I am afraid that just as Eve was deceived by the serpent's cunning, your minds may somehow be led astray from your sincere and pure devotion to Christ.*

We are being led astray by Satan, who is controlling Hollywood. We jump when they say jump and we support so much that we should not. We see and listen to what they call good, but we disobey God by accepting their morals instead of standing up for His.

GODLY PRINCIPLES

I Corinthians 3:16: *Don't you know that you yourselves are God's temple and that God's Spirit lives in you?*

PRINCIPLE: IF WE WOULD NOT SHOW IT, READ IT, OR LISTEN TO IT IN CHURCH, THEN IT SHOULD NOT BE ALLOWED IN OUR TEMPLE. GUARD YOUR HEARTS.

> ***2 John 1:7–11:*** *Many deceivers, who do not acknowledge Jesus Christ as coming in the flesh, have gone out into the world. Any such person is the deceiver and the antichrist. Watch out that you do not lose what you have worked for, but that you may be rewarded fully. Anyone who runs ahead and does not continue in the teaching of Christ does not have God; whoever continues in the teaching has both the Father and the Son. If anyone comes to you and does not bring this teaching, do not take him into your house or welcome him. Anyone who welcomes him shares in his wicked work.*

The context of this passage is that many deceivers have gone out to lead people astray. In their day, it was traveling preachers, but in our day we allow teachings into our home that do not bring the teachings of Christ through the TV, radios, books, magazines, etc. If someone comes into your home and you have a dirty magazine on the coffee table you would, hopefully, be embarrassed, but do you have movies that have sexual immorality in them? Are they displayed around your entertainment center? If your child came into the room and said a curse word while you had company over, hopefully, you would be offended, but do you have movies that have curse words in them displayed proudly in your collection? Would you be honored to sit down with Jesus and watch every movie that you own?

PRINCIPLE: WHEN WE BRING THINGS (MOVIES, MAGAZINES, MUSIC, ETC.) INTO OUR HOMES THAT DO NOT BRING THE TEACHINGS OF CHRIST, WE ARE SHARING IN THEIR WICKED WORK.

I Peter 1:14–15: As obedient children, do not conform to the evil desires you had when you lived in ignorance. But just as he who called you is holy, so be holy in all you do.

PRINCIPLE: HOLINESS IN THE BIBLE MEANS SEPARATION FROM <u>ALL</u> THAT IS COMMON OR UNCLEAN. IN RESPECT TO GOD, HOLINESS MEANS THAT HE IS SEPARATE FROM ALL THAT IS UNCLEAN AND EVIL (*Basic Theology: A Popular Systematic Guide to Understanding Biblical Truth*)

We are to be aliens and strangers in this world. We are to be living for heaven and not clinging to the things of this world. Sin will not be in heaven. God cannot be around our worldly movie, music, and book collections. Why then do we have it? How are we being holy by participating and supporting things that are evil and will not be in heaven?

WHY ALL OF THE TEMPTATIONS?

Deuteronomy 13:1–4: If a prophet, or one who foretells by dreams, appears among you and announces to you a miraculous sign or wonder, and if the sign or wonder of which he has spoken takes place, and he says, "Let us follow other gods" (gods you have not known) "and let us worship them," you must not listen to the words of that prophet or dreamer. The LORD your God is testing you to find out whether you love him with all your heart and with all your soul. It is the LORD your God you must follow, and him you must revere. Keep his commands and obey him; serve him and hold fast to him.

God does not want robots. He wants and He deserves true worship. He is such an awesome, loving God that He desires to be worshiped by those that have a choice to worship Him. God could have created us in such a way that we would constantly worship Him and we would not have an option to not worship Him, but that would make us robots and not true worshipers. To have a true worshiper there must be an option and that option must be hard. Remember that even in the Garden there was a choice.

> **Deuteronomy 8:16–20:** *He gave you manna to eat in the desert, something your fathers had never known, to humble and to test you so that in the end it might go well with you. You may say to yourself, "My power and the strength of my hands have produced this wealth for me." But remember the LORD your God, for it is he who gives you the ability to produce wealth, and so confirms his covenant, which he swore to your forefathers, as it is today. If you ever forget the LORD your God and follow other gods and worship and bow down to them, I testify against you today that you will surely be destroyed. Like the nations the LORD destroyed before you, so you will be destroyed for not obeying the LORD your God.*

OUR PROBLEM

We are all sinners, all of us has turned away (Romans 3). If we do not allow the Holy Spirit to enable and help us to be holy, we will turn away and be destroyed like the nations before us as Romans 3:20 points out.

THE SOLUTION: JESUS

> **Romans 3:22–26:** *This righteousness from God comes through faith in Jesus Christ to all who believe. There is no difference, for all have sinned and fall short of the glory of God, and are justified freely by his grace through the redemption that came by Christ Jesus. God presented him as a sacrifice of atonement, through faith in his blood. He did this to demonstrate his justice, because in his forbearance he had left the sins committed beforehand unpunished—he did it to*

demonstrate his justice at the present time, so as to be just and the one who justifies those who have faith in Jesus.

THE MISUNDERSTANDING OF OUR DAY

Jesus did not die on the cross and save us from our sins in order for us to continue to live in them. He died on the cross to set us free from our sinful ways and desires.

> *Titus 2:11–12: For the grace of God that brings salvation has appeared to all men. It teaches us to say "No" to ungodliness and worldly passions, and to live self-controlled, upright and godly lives in this present age.*

The call of God on our life is to become more holy, and it is the grace of God that teaches us how. Many times we twist the grace of God and we use it for a license for immorality. Jude speaks about this misunderstanding as well. We are not saved by grace to remain in our sin, we are saved and then God brings us out of the unclean and sinful.

> *Romans 8:3–4: For what the law was powerless to do in that it was weakened by the sinful nature, God did by sending his own Son in the likeness of sinful man to be a sin offering. And so he condemned sin in sinful man, in order that the righteous requirements of the law might be fully met in us, who do not live according to the sinful nature but according to the Spirit.*

The righteous requirements of the law were exemplified by the life that Jesus lived. We are called to follow Him and live as He lived upon this earth. The questions then become: Would Jesus own this movie? Would Jesus go and support this movie? Would he listen to the same radio station that I do? Whatever He would or would not do becomes our standard. If it is holy, He would be a part of it. If it is unholy then He would abstain from it.

2 Corinthians 6:14–18: *Do not be yoked together with unbelievers. For what do righteousness and wickedness have in common? Or what fellowship can light have with darkness? What harmony is there between Christ and Belial? What does a believer have in common with an unbeliever? What agreement is there between the temple of God and idols? For we are the temple of the living God. As God has said: "I will live with them and walk among them, and I will be their God, and they will be my people." "Therefore come out from them and be separate, says the Lord. Touch no unclean thing, and I will receive you." "I will be a Father to you, and you will be my sons and daughters, says the Lord Almighty."*

We many times use this passage to teach believers that they are not to be married to an unbeliever. That teaching is fine, but it is not the context. The context is that we are to not be yoked with unbelievers at all. We are not to be led by them. To be under the yoke of Christ is to submit to His leadership and His teachings. To be yoked with an unbeliever is to listen to their advice and teachings. Again, Satan is in control of most of the media and he is teaching us to disobey God. We need to be aware of his schemes and begin to come out from them and be separate. If God says that taking his name in vain is a sin, yet, the world says that it is okay, whom are we to listen to? You might say, "Well I agree that taking His name in vain is a sin, but it is all right for me to own or watch movies that take His name in vain." Why would it be all right? Jesus would not own or watch such a movie, so why is it all right for us?

WAR, SELF-DENIAL, AND SUFFERING

1 Peter 2:11: *Dear friends, I urge you, as aliens and strangers in the world, to abstain from sinful desires, which war against your soul.*

Where is the self-denial? Where is the internal war that Paul speaks about? Many Christians suffer with addictions and depression. They continually go under and wonder why they cannot be free. If you continually stay in the deep end of the pool, eventually, you are going to become tired and you are going to go under, but if you move to the shallow end and eventually get out of the pool you will experience more power in your life. The pool symbolizes the world and its influence on our lives. Getting out of the pool symbolizes what the Lord has asked of us. Come out from them and be separate. Stop listening to their advice, it will only feed your flesh and it will eventually pull you under again. Continually feed yourself upon the Word of God and watch His power in your life.

> *I Peter 4:1–4:* *Therefore, since Christ suffered in his body, arm yourselves also with the same attitude, because he who has suffered in his body is done with sin. As a result, he does not live the rest of his earthly life for evil human desires, but rather for the will of God. For you have spent enough time in the past doing what pagans choose to do—living in debauchery, lust, drunkenness, orgies, carousing and detestable idolatry. They think it strange that you do not plunge with them into the same flood of dissipation, and they heap abuse on you.*

Are we willing to suffer for Christ? Are we willing to deny our desires to be entertained and seek His call to be holy? There are so many Scriptures that teach us how we are to deny ourselves, pick up our cross, put to death our desires, and follow Him. In this transformation we experience freedom, security, and God's blessings.

> *Mark 8:34–35:* *Then he called the crowd to him along with his disciples and said: "If anyone would come after me, he must deny himself and take up his cross and follow me. For whoever wants to save his life will lose it, but whoever loses his life for me and for the gospel will save it."*

> *Romans 8:12–13:* *Therefore, brothers, we have an obligation—but it is not to the sinful nature, to live according to*

it. For if you live according to the sinful nature, you will die; but if by the Spirit you put to death the misdeeds of the body, you will live.

Galatians 5:16–21: *So I say, live by the Spirit, and you will not gratify the desires of the sinful nature. For the sinful nature desires what is contrary to the Spirit, and the Spirit what is contrary to the sinful nature. They are in conflict with each other, so that you do not do what you want. But if you are led by the Spirit, you are not under law. The acts of the sinful nature are obvious: sexual immorality, impurity and debauchery; idolatry and witchcraft; hatred, discord, jealousy, fits of rage, selfish ambition, dissensions, factions and envy; drunkenness, orgies, and the like. I warn you, as I did before, that those who live like this will not inherit the kingdom of God.*

In your inner self, you can feel the conflict building. You know what God's Word says; yet you battle with the fleshly desires to please yourself. It is only through Christ that we can overcome and live by the Spirit. It is a must. In the Old Testament we read how the nations before us turned away from God and experienced His judgments and curses. The New Testament warns us as well. If we live to please ourselves, we will reap destruction, but if we live to please the Spirit, we will reap eternal life. What would Jesus listen to, watch, read, or have in His home?

I John 2:6: *Whoever claims to live in him must walk as Jesus did.*

ABSTAIN FROM IMMORALITY

I commit that I will abstain from whatever presents immorality as acceptable. I will be aware of Satan's tricks and I will stand up for God's morals. I will get rid of the moral filth, based upon God's Word, that I have allowed into my life and I will be holy to the Lord. (Deuteronomy 7:26; 8:10–14; I John 5:19; Ephesians 2:2; 5:3–7; 2 John 2:7–11; James 1:21; Exodus 20:7; Colossians 3:8; I Peter 2:11; I John 1:8, 9)

LESSON TWO
MAKE PRAYER AND GOD'S WORD A PRIORITY

THE CURSE OF NOT HEEDING GOD'S WORD

Deuteronomy 6:4–9: Hear, O Israel: The LORD our God, the LORD is one. Love the LORD your God with all your heart and with all your soul and with all your strength. These commandments that I give you today are to be upon your hearts._____ (1) them on your children. Talk about them when you sit at home and when you walk along the road, when you lie down and when you get up. Tie them as symbols on your hands and bind them on your foreheads. Write them on the doorframes of your houses and on your gates.

If I gave out two tests, one based upon biblical knowledge and the other based upon "Hollywood" knowledge, which test would you pass?

THE POWER OF GOD'S WORD

2 Timothy 3:14–17: But as for you, continue in what you have learned and have become convinced of, because you know those from whom you learned it, and how from infancy you have known the holy Scriptures, which are able to make you wise for salvation through faith in Christ Jesus. All Scripture is _____ (2) and is useful for teaching, rebuking, correcting and training in righteousness, so that the man of God may be thoroughly equipped for every good work.

Psalm 119:11: I have _____ (3) your word in my heart that I might not sin against you.

As a parent, which way are you leading your children? Do they know the Holy Scriptures which are able to make them "wise for salvation"? Are they hiding God's Word in their hearts in order for them not to sin against God?

THERE IS LIFE IN HIS WORD

> **Deuteronomy 32:45–47:** *When Moses finished reciting all these words to all Israel, he said to them, "Take to heart all the words I have solemnly declared to you this day, so that you may command your children to obey carefully all the words of this law. They are not just idle words for you—they are your _____ (4). By them you will live long in the land you are crossing the Jordan to possess."*

> **Matthew 4:4:** *Jesus answered, "It is written: 'Man does not live on bread alone, but on every _____ (5) that comes from the mouth of God.'"*

> **Hebrews 4:12:** *For the word of God is _____ (6) and active. Sharper than any double-edged sword, it penetrates even to dividing soul and spirit, joints and marrow; it judges the thoughts and attitudes of the heart.*

God's Word will not return void; it will accomplish its work in you, but you have to _____ (7) to it.

THERE IS POWER IN PRAYER

> **I John 1:8–9:** *If we claim to be without sin, we deceive ourselves and the truth is not in us. If we confess our sins, he is faithful and just and will forgive us our sins and purify us from all unrighteousness.*

One of the most amazing things to me in our relationship with God is the fact that we are just a _____ (8) away from being right with God.

Luke 11:9–13: So I say to you: Ask and it will be given to you; seek and you will find; knock and the door will be opened to you. For everyone who asks receives; he who seeks finds; and to him who knocks, the door will be opened. Which of you fathers, if your son asks for a fish, will give him a snake instead? Or if he asks for an egg, will give him a scorpion? If you then, though you are evil, know how to give good gifts to your children, how much more will your Father in heaven give the _____ _____ (9) to those who ask him!

We are losing our children to the enemy, and we are too busy worrying about our entertainment to care about the lost souls of men. Shouldn't we be having prayer meetings all across our country for the lost souls of men? Shouldn't we be having prayer meetings for the many Christian children that have turned away from the faith?

RELATIONSHIP IS THE KEY

God wants each of us to be in an intimate relationship with Him. He wants to speak _____ (10) to you.

FOR GOD TO HEAL OUR LAND, WE MUST TURN BACK TO HIM

_____ (11) ourselves. (Admit our sin and need for Him)

_____ (12). (Ask for forgiveness)

Seek His face. (Search the Scriptures, Relationship)

_____ (13) from our wicked ways. (Repent)

WHAT NEXT? PURGE THE EVIL FROM AMONG YOU

Judges 10:15–16: But the Israelites said to the LORD, "We have sinned. Do with us whatever you think best, but please rescue us now." Then they _____ _____ (14) *of the foreign gods among them and served the LORD. And he could bear Israel's misery no longer.*

1 Samuel 7:3–4: And Samuel said to the whole house of Israel, "If you are returning to the LORD with all your hearts, then _____ (15) yourselves of the foreign gods and the Ashtoreths and commit yourselves to the LORD and serve him only, and he will deliver you out of the hand of the Philistines." So the Israelites put away their Baals and Ashtoreths, and served the LORD only.

Ezekiel 20:7: And I said to them, "Each of you, _____ _____ (16) of the vile images you have set your eyes on, and do not defile yourselves with the idols of Egypt. I am the LORD your God."

Do you see that time and time again the nation would slowly be desensitized by sin and when they returned to God, they got rid of their idols? What is in your home that needs to be gotten rid of?

Deuteronomy 7:26: Do not bring a detestable thing into your _____ (17) or you, like it, will be set apart for destruction. Utterly abhor and detest it, for it is set apart for destruction.

Since God is holy and He cannot be around sin, then anything that goes against His righteousness would be detestable. A movie that has only one curse word, a movie that takes His name in vain only one time would be considered detestable. The New Testament brings these same teachings into our lives as well.

2 John 1:9–11: Anyone who runs ahead and does not continue in the teaching of Christ does not have God; whoever continues in the teaching has both the Father and the Son. If anyone comes to you and does not bring this teaching, do not take him into your _____ (18) or welcome him.

Anyone who welcomes him shares in his wicked work.

We not only welcome immorality into our homes, but we display it proudly right next to our greatest idol, the TV.

ARE WE HELPING THE CAUSE OF EVIL?

> ***James 4:4:*** *You adulterous people, don't you know that friendship with the world is hatred toward God? Anyone who chooses to be a friend of the world becomes an _____ (19) of God.*

Let's open up our eyes to the bigger picture and stop looking for immediate gratification. There are consequences to our actions, and we must realize that we will be held accountable in how we handle the money the Lord has entrusted to us. Take action and begin to rid your life of the moral filth that you have acquired. Realize what you are really supporting.

> ***James 1:21:*** *Therefore, _____ _____ (20) of all moral filth and the evil that is so prevalent and humbly accept the word planted in you, which can save you.*

Remember: Obedience equals blessings.

SANCTIFICATION

The process to be holy is called sanctification. It is hard and it takes time, but everything that you own is God's and it must be sanctified. We must stop justifying what we allow in our lives and we must start asking the question, is it _____ (21)?

> ***Galatians 5:17:*** *For the sinful nature desires what is contrary to the Spirit, and the Spirit what is contrary to the sinful nature. They are in conflict with each other, so that you do not do what you _____ (22).*

Colossians 3:8: But now you must rid yourselves of . . . filthy language from your lips.

Exodus 20:7: You shall not misuse the name of the LORD your God, for the LORD will not hold anyone guiltless who misuses his name.

PRINCIPLE: SINCE GOD CANNNOT BE AROUND ANY SIN, THEN A MOVIE THAT HAS JUST ONE CURSE WORD WILL NOT BE ALLOWED IN HEAVEN. IF IT WILL NOT BE ALLOWED IN HEAVEN, SHOULD IT BE ALLOWED IN OUR _____ (23) OR SANCTIFIED HOME?

THINGS TO SANCTIFY

Your television programs / iPods / mp3 players / books / magazines / movie collections / video games / your car stereo / your cell phones / whatever else that would be contrary to God's standards

Remember: Whatever presents immorality as _____ (24) is what we abstain from.

EXAMPLE: Some movies that have immoralities in them would be okay to watch. For instance, the movie *The Passion of the Christ* depicts great immorality, but it does not use foul language to get the point across. The immorality is also not presented as acceptable. To watch a movie that has redeeming qualities and Christ as the source of the redemption is biblical. There are many immoralities presented to us from the Scriptures, but none of them are presented as acceptable.

REPLACE YOUR LOST TIME

† Begin to replace your time in the world with Godly things.
† Begin having a quiet time again.
† Begin having family devotions.
† Begin reading a chapter a day in the Bible.

† Begin having family nights.

WARNING: Because of the moral decay of the church there are many Bible studies based upon ungodly movies. Also, remember that just because a movie is sold in a Christian bookstore it no longer means that it does not have any immoralities in it. A good resource for movies is ***http://christianmovies.com.***Some of them are older movies, but they will not have any immoralities presented as acceptable.

MAKE PRAYER AND GOD'S WORD A PRIORITY

I will make prayer and God's Word a priority in my life and my family's life. I will discipline myself to my quiet times, and I will make opportunities where we read and pray together as a couple or family. (Matthew 4:4; Psalm 1:1; 119:11; Deuteronomy 6:4–9; 32:45–47; I Thessalonians 5:17; Hebrews 4:12)

BEFORE LESSON 3 READ THROUGH:

COMMITMENT TWO   *48*

COMMITMENT 2
MAKE PRAYER AND
GOD'S WORD A PRIORITY

THE SECOND COMMITMENT:
MAKE PRAYER AND GOD'S WORD A PRIORITY

I will make prayer and God's Word a priority in my life and my family's life. I will discipline myself to my quiet times, and I will make opportunities where we read and pray together as a couple or family. (Matthew 4:4; Psalm 1:1; 119:11; Deuteronomy 6:4–9; 32:45–47; 1 Thessalonians 5:17; Hebrews 4:12)

THE CURSE OF NOT HEEDING GOD'S WORD

> **Deuteronomy 6:4–9:** *Hear, O Israel: The LORD our God, the LORD is one. Love the LORD your God with all your heart and with all your soul and with all your strength. These commandments that I give you today are to be upon your hearts. Impress them on your children. Talk about them when you sit at home and when you walk along the road, when you lie down and when you get up. Tie them as symbols on your hands and bind them on your foreheads. Write them on the doorframes of your houses and on your gates.*

If I gave out two tests, one based upon biblical knowledge and the other based upon "Hollywood" knowledge, which test would you pass? Do you enjoy watching Hollywood gossip shows more than reading God's Word? Could you answer more *Trivial Pursuit* questions than *Bible Trivia*? Is it true that you can talk about the latest movies, television shows, and sporting events, but you have a hard time naming the great people of faith in Hebrews 11? Many churches across our country have trivia nights, and they are turning away from *Bible Trivia* because the people of God no longer know God's Word. **Shouldn't the people of God be able to play *Bible Trivia* without feeling dumb?** God has called us to heed His Word. He has called us to teach it, memorize it, and obey it. Would you say we are doing a good job of that in the home? Most Christian families do not read the Word or pray together outside of repeating the dinner table prayer night after night.

THE POWER OF GOD'S WORD

2 Timothy 3:14–17: *But as for you, continue in what you have learned and have become convinced of, because you know those from whom you learned it, and how from infancy you have known the holy Scriptures, which are able to make you wise for salvation through faith in Christ Jesus. All Scripture is God-breathed and is useful for teaching, rebuking, correcting and training in righteousness, so that the man of God may be thoroughly equipped for every good work.*

Psalm 119:11: *I have hidden your word in my heart that I might not sin against you.*

As a parent, which way are you leading your children? Do they know the Holy Scriptures which are able to make them "wise for salvation" (2 Timothy 3:15)? Are they hiding God's Word in their hearts in order for them not to sin against God? Do they ever see you reading God's Word? Do they ever see you praying? Do you ever read the Bible together? What do they see you doing? Do they see you watching TV, going to sporting events, going to the movies, or working many long hours to make money?

THERE IS LIFE IN HIS WORD

Deuteronomy 32:45–47: *When Moses finished reciting all these words to all Israel, he said to them, "Take to heart all the words I have solemnly declared to you this day, so that you may command your children to obey carefully all the words of this law. They are not just idle words for you—they are your life. By them you will live long in the land you are crossing the Jordan to possess."*

Matthew 4:4: *Jesus answered, "It is written: 'Man does not live on bread alone, but on every word that comes from the mouth of God.'"*

Isaiah 55:11: *So is my word that goes out from my mouth: It will not return to me empty, but will accomplish what I desire and achieve the purpose for which I sent it.*

Hebrews 4:12: *For the word of God is living and active. Sharper than any double-edged sword, it penetrates even to dividing soul and spirit, joints and marrow; it judges the thoughts and attitudes of the heart.*

God's Word will not return void; it will accomplish its work in you, but you have to commit to it. When a seed is planted, it does not sprout up at once. It takes time. It takes nurture, care, and consistency. A good gardener will tell you that to reap the best crops, you need to water at the same time every day and be consistent in caring for the plants. God's Word is living and active. It will penetrate and begin to build a root system in you. A seed begins to grow a root system under the ground where no one can see before it produces fruit that people can see. So it is with you. Even though you do not see or feel any fruit, you can be assured that God is building a root system in you preparing you to be a mighty tree that can withstand the storms of life. You will eventually see fruit; do not give up. Sow seeds of obedience.

Sometimes people tell me that they do not feel close to God, and I ask them, "Have you been reading His Word? Have you been praying? Have you been surrendering to Him as your Lord?" If you are not reading, you are starving your spirit. Sometimes people confess to me that they are struggling with an addiction, and I ask them, "Are you memorizing Scripture? Are you seeking after Jesus to heal and free you?" As spoiled Americans, we want the easy way out, but God is testing us to see if we want Him more than the things of this world. Will you "work out your salvation" as Philippians 2:12 tells us? Will you abstain from your desires and seek God?

THERE IS POWER IN PRAYER

I John 1:8–9: *If we claim to be without sin, we deceive ourselves and the truth is not in us. If we confess our sins, he is faithful and just and will forgive us our sins and purify us from all unrighteousness.*

One of the most amazing things to me in our relationship with God is the fact that we are just a prayer away from being right with God. No matter what sin we have committed, we can come to God through Christ. The importance of our prayer is the attitude of our heart. Are we willing to turn from our sins? Are we willing to repent? As you progress through this book, keep an attitude of prayer and keep asking the Holy Spirit to reveal to you what you need to repent from. Ask the Holy Spirit to give you the strength and the self-discipline to abstain from immoralities. Hear His voice through His Word.

Luke 11:9–13: *So I say to you: Ask and it will be given to you; seek and you will find; knock and the door will be opened to you. For everyone who asks receives; he who seeks finds; and to him who knocks, the door will be opened. Which of you fathers, if your son asks for a fish, will give him a snake instead? Or if he asks for an egg, will give him a scorpion? If you then, though you are evil, know how to give good gifts to your children, how much more will your Father in heaven give the Holy Spirit to those who ask him!*

We need to begin fighting in the spiritual warfare that is going on around us. We are losing our children to the enemy, and we are too busy worrying about our entertainment to care about the lost souls of men. Shouldn't we be having prayer meetings all across our country for the lost souls of men? Shouldn't we be having prayer meetings for the many Christian children that have turned away from the faith?

RELATIONSHIP IS THE KEY

God wants each of us to be in an intimate relationship with Him. He wants to speak personally to you. He wants you to listen carefully to Him and to His Word. It would not be right for me to tell you what you can watch and what you cannot watch. It would not help you in your relationship with God for me to tell you what to do and not to do. You must have a relationship with the Lord. You need to hear His voice on the matter. You need to be repenting because He is your Lord and you desire to live your life in such a way as to give Him glory. It is right for me to present to you the biblical standard and then to call you to abide by it.

FOR GOD TO HEAL OUR LAND, WE MUST TURN BACK TO HIM

Humble ourselves. (Admit our sin and need for Him)

Pray. (Ask for forgiveness)

Seek His face. (Search the Scriptures, Relationship)

Turn from our wicked ways. (Repent)

WHAT NEXT? PURGE THE EVIL FROM AMONG YOU

In the Old Testament the nation would go through the Deuteronomic cycle, as we are, and they would get to the point where they realized their sin. They would realize that they had gotten away from God's law and that they had allowed things of this world into their lives and homes. They would either repent and turn back to God, or they would continue in their sin and go further into slavery. Do we really want the world to take our Bibles away? Do we really want to have to go into hiding just to have a worship service? Let's purge the evil from among us, cry out to God, and hope that it is not too late.

The nation of Israel struggled to keep the snares of Satan out of their community. The people around them would create idols that would tempt them to run after them. They looked so appealing, and they seemed to be working for the people around them. The nations around them would worship these idols and ask them to produce rain, and it looked like rain would come. They would ask the idols for children, and it looked like children would come. Why would God allow the rain and children to come? He did it to test them, to see if they would run after the ways of the world instead of choosing Him. Once the nation realized that they had sinned and allowed the idolatries into their homes, they would get rid of them. Satan has slipped in again and tricked us to follow the ways of this world. He has tempted us and gradually gotten us to accept immoralities that the generations before us would have been appalled at. We have been desensitized, and we have placed these immoralities into our homes as well. Look at what the nations before us did when they realized their sin.

> **Judges 10:15–16:** *But the Israelites said to the LORD, "We have sinned. Do with us whatever you think best, but please rescue us now." Then they got rid of the foreign gods among them and served the LORD. And he could bear Israel's misery no longer.*

> **I Samuel 7:3–4:** *And Samuel said to the whole house of Israel, "If you are returning to the LORD with all your hearts, then rid yourselves of the foreign gods and the Ashtoreths and commit yourselves to the LORD and serve him only, and he will deliver you out of the hand of the Philistines." So the Israelites put away their Baals and Ashtoreths, and served the LORD only.*

> **Ezekiel 20:7:** *And I said to them, "Each of you, get rid of the vile images you have set your eyes on, and do not defile yourselves with the idols of Egypt. I am the LORD your God."*

Do you see the pattern? Do you see that time and time again the nation would slowly be desensitized by sin and when they returned to God, they got rid of their idols? What is in your home that needs to be gotten rid of?

> **Deuteronomy 7:26:** *Do not bring a detestable thing into your house or you, like it, will be set apart for destruction. Utterly abhor and detest it, for it is set apart for destruction.*

Since God is holy and He cannot be around sin, then anything that goes against His righteousness would be detestable. A movie that has only one curse word, a movie that takes His name in vain only one time would be considered detestable. The New Testament brings these same teachings into our lives as well.

> **2 John 1:9–11:** *Anyone who runs ahead and does not continue in the teaching of Christ does not have God; whoever continues in the teaching has both the Father and the Son. If anyone comes to you and does not bring this teaching, do not take him into your house or welcome him. Anyone who welcomes him shares in his wicked work.*

Do we really want to share in the judgment of the wicked? We not only welcome immorality into our homes, but we display it proudly right next to our greatest idol, the TV. If Jesus owned a TV, what would He watch? If Jesus had a DVD collection, would it resemble yours? Would Jesus have an entertainment center that resembles yours? If the glory of God came into your home, what would remain? God is a consuming fire and His fire will burn up all that is sinful. Sin cannot be in the presence of the almighty God. So again, if God's glory came into your home what would remain? What should you get rid of? What if the glory of God came into your iPod, or your mp3 player, etc., what would remain?

ARE WE HELPING THE CAUSE OF EVIL?

I love to get lost in a good movie. It helps me relax and not worry about the issues surrounding me, but does my entertainment choice have consequences that I cannot even see? It does when I am sending my money to something that God would call evil. William Federer calls the Deuteronomic cycle "the cycle of nations." When the nations would wander away from God, He would allow them to go into slavery. Another nation would rise up, and God would allow that nation to overpower them. Federer says that "in this cycle God would allow the Hittites, Amorites, Mosquito Bites, Bud Lites, and whatever other ites the Lord chose to awaken His people to their disobedience." Perhaps we should support only what Jesus would support and stop compromising His standards.

> *James 4:4:* *You adulterous people, don't you know that friendship with the world is hatred toward God? Anyone who chooses to be a friend of the world becomes an enemy of God.*

Let's open up our eyes to the bigger picture and stop looking for immediate gratification. There are consequences to our actions, and we must realize that we will be held accountable in how we handle the money the Lord has entrusted to us. Take action and begin to rid your life of the moral filth that you have acquired. Realize what you are really supporting.

> *James 1:21:* *Therefore, get rid of all moral filth and the evil that is so prevalent and humbly accept the word planted in you, which can save you.*

Remember: Obedience equals blessings. Your repentance will be rewarded if you are doing it to bring glory to God. Peace, joy, assurance, and clarity will be part of your life.

SANCTIFICATION

The process to be holy is called sanctification. It is hard and it takes time, but everything that you own is God's and it must be sanctified. It is hard because we still have a flesh that desires to do evil. Our flesh desires to have and do things that are against God. We must learn to live by the Spirit and not to gratify our sinful desires. Remember, just because it is funny or we enjoy it does not make it right or moral. Only God's Word dictates what is right and moral. We must stop justifying what we allow in our lives and we must start asking the question, is it holy?

> **Galatians 5:17:** *For the sinful nature desires what is contrary to the Spirit, and the Spirit what is contrary to the sinful nature. They are in conflict with each other, so that you do not do what you want.*

> **Colossians 3:8:** *But now you must rid yourselves of . . . filthy language from your lips.*

> **Exodus 20:7:** *You shall not misuse the name of the LORD your God, for the LORD will not hold anyone guiltless who misuses his name.*

As you begin to go through all of your possessions to make them obedient to Christ, you need to remember to pray and ask for strength. You need to remember to use God's Word as the standard and not your flesh.

A good principle to go by: SINCE GOD CANNNOT BE AROUND ANY SIN, THEN A MOVIE THAT HAS JUST ONE CURSE WORD WILL NOT BE ALLOWED IN HEAVEN. IF IT WILL NOT BE ALLOWED IN HEAVEN, SHOULD IT BE ALLOWED IN OUR TEMPLE OR SANCTIFIED HOME?

THINGS TO SANCTIFY

Your television programs / iPods / mp3 players / books / magazines / movie collections / video games / your car stereo / your cell phones / whatever else that would be contrary to God's standards

Remember: Whatever presents immorality as acceptable is what we abstain from.

EXAMPLE: Some movies that have immoralities in them would be okay to watch. For instance, the movie *The Passion of the Christ* depicts great immorality, but it does not use foul language to get the point across. The immorality is also not presented as acceptable. To watch a movie that has redeeming qualities and Christ as the source of the redemption is biblical. There are many immoralities presented to us from the Scriptures, but none of them are presented as acceptable.

PERSONAL NOTE: As a parent you need to be teaching your children how to apply the Word. Teach them why you are getting rid of things. Show them the Scriptures that detail the snares of our world. Pray together and ask the Lord for wisdom. Use the above principle questions to define what should and should not be allowed in your homes and lives. Allow teenagers to make certain choices outside of the home but not in it. As a parent you will be held responsible for what you have allowed in the home. You will be responsible for sharing in the wicked work if you allow it. As you begin to apply God's Word to your daily life and make choices that honor Him, you will begin to hear His voice. Listen to Him. Allow Him to teach you what it means to walk with Him and live in the light.

Don't just watch and listen to things that could be considered moral by God's standards. Too many movies or songs that could be considered moral but do not have redemptive qualities can lead to the deception that good people go to heaven. We need to remember that everyone is a sinner and without the blood of Jesus covering our sins, we will end up in hell. We need to be passionate about seeking to save the lost and not just focused upon finding moral entertainment.

REPLACE YOUR LOST TIME

Most of us have spent so much time chasing after the things of this world that we will have a lot of free time if we keep our commitment. Begin to replace your time in the world with Godly things.

Begin having a quiet time again. Go to a Christian bookstore and get a good Bible study like *Masterlife*, or *Experiencing God*, or a Beth Moore study.

Begin having family devotions. There are many resources to choose from.

Begin reading a chapter a day in the Bible.

Begin having family nights. Play games, but be careful of the games you choose, some are not sanctified. Watch a Christian movie. Go hiking or riding bikes, or enjoy another God-pleasing activity.

WARNING: Because of the moral decay of the church there are many Bible studies based upon ungodly movies. Also, remember that just because a movie is sold in a Christian bookstore it no longer means that it does not have any immoralities in it. A good resource for movies is ***http://christianmovies.com.***Some of them are older movies, but they will not have any immoralities presented as acceptable.

MAKE PRAYER AND GOD'S WORD A PRIORITY

I will make prayer and God's Word a priority in my life and my family's life. I will discipline myself to my quiet times, and I will make opportunities where we read and pray together as a couple or family. (Matthew 4:4; Psalm 1:1; 119:11; Deuteronomy 6:4–9; 32:45–47; 1 Thessalonians 5:17; Hebrews 4:12)

LESSON THREE
HONOR THE SABBATH

* _____ (1) percent of students from "Christian" homes deny their faith before they graduate from college.
* **91 percent of students from evangelical churches do not believe in absolute moral truth (http://codebluerally.com/info.php).**

The statistics should _____ (2) us. What are we doing wrong?

> *Exodus 20:8–11: Remember the Sabbath day by keeping it holy. Six days you shall labor and do all your work, but the seventh day is a Sabbath to the LORD your God. On it you shall not do any work, neither you, nor your son or daughter, nor your manservant or maidservant, nor your animals, nor the alien within your gates. For in six days the LORD made the heavens and the earth, the sea, and all that is in them, but he rested on the seventh day. Therefore the LORD blessed the Sabbath day and made it _____ (3).*

> *Exodus 31:12–17: Then the LORD said to Moses, "Say to the Israelites, 'You must observe my Sabbaths. This will be a _____ (4) between me and you for the generations to come, so you may know that I am the LORD, who makes you holy. Observe the Sabbath, because it is holy to you. Anyone who desecrates it must be put to death; whoever does any work on that day must be cut off from his people. For six days, work is to be done, but the seventh day is a Sabbath of rest, holy to the LORD. Whoever does any work on the Sabbath day must be put to death. The Israelites are to observe the Sabbath, celebrating it for the generations to come as a lasting*

covenant. It will be a sign between me and the Israelites forever, for in six days the LORD made the heavens and the earth, and on the seventh day he abstained from work and rested.'"

FROM SATURDAY TO SUNDAY

The seventh day that God rested on was Saturday, but after the Lord was resurrected on Sunday, the church began to honor the Sabbath on Sunday, the first day of the week. This became known as the Lord's Day.

> ***Acts 20:7:*** *On the _____ (5) day of the week we came together to break bread. Paul spoke to the people and, because he intended to leave the next day, kept on talking until midnight.*

> ***Revelation 1:10:*** *On the Lord's Day I was in the Spirit, and I heard behind me a loud voice like a trumpet.*

When our country was founded upon God's principles and laws we continued to honor the Lord's Day and we took seriously the Scriptures about the Sabbath. Today, we are desecrating the Lord's Day.

PUTTING GOD FIRST IN OUR LIVES

Many Christians would respond that God is first in their lives, but their _____ (6) may be saying something different. For example, let's say that you are a member of a church and that you attend church most of the time, but there are some Sundays that you miss. You miss for hunting, vacation, professional sporting events (live or on TV), your child's practice or game, a concert, a movie, a television show, or just because you feel like staying home.

When we miss church for _____ (7) reasons, aren't we telling the world that God is first in our lives unless something better comes along?

> *Isaiah 58:13–14:* "*If you keep your feet from breaking the Sabbath and from doing as you please on my holy day, if you call the Sabbath a delight and the LORD'S holy day honorable, and if you honor it by not going your_____ (8) way and not doing as you please or speaking idle words, then you will find your joy in the LORD, and I will cause you to ride on the heights of the land and to feast on the inheritance of your father Jacob.*" *The mouth of the LORD has spoken.*

> *Isaiah 56:2:* *Blessed is the man who does this, the man who holds it fast, who keeps the _____ (9) without desecrating it, and keeps his hand from doing any evil.*

SOWING SEEDS OF DOUBT

Have you ever arrived at church and wondered where your friends are? If they missed church for _____ (10) reasons, you were most likely disappointed and discouraged, maybe even irritated.

IT IS NO COINCIDENCE

Satan has a goal and he knows how to achieve his purposes. He is very crafty. He knew that when television came out, he could not show the things that are on today all at once. He desensitized us a little at a time. He has done the same with the _____ (11).

THE BLUE LAW

The blue law is a type of law typically found in the United States and designed to enforce moral standards, particularly the observance of _____ (12) as a day of worship or rest, and restrict Sunday shopping.

In America the law was changed in the 1980s.

Even though man's law says it's okay, is that enough to break God's law? Who is leading whom?

THE RETURN OF GOD'S POWER

Are you sick and tired of being ridiculed for your faith? Are you tired of the media cutting us down and saying that we are narrow minded? Then repent and allow God to glorify Himself through you! Turn back to the principles that our country was _____ (13) upon and watch God do some amazing things.

HOW TO DEFINE WORK

> *Exodus 20:9–10: Six days you shall labor and do all your work, but the seventh day is a Sabbath to the LORD your God. On it you shall not do _____ (14) work, neither you, nor your son or daughter, nor your manservant or maidservant, nor your animals, nor the alien within your gates.*

What can we do and not do on the Sabbath?

I believe that missing church for anything other than an emergency or sickness is wrong.

> *Hebrews 10:25: Let us not give up meeting _____ (15), as some are in the habit of doing, but let us encourage one another—and all the more as you see the Day approaching.*

> *Romans 8:3–4: For what the law was powerless to do in that it was weakened by the sinful nature, God did by sending his own Son in the likeness of sinful man to be a sin offering. And so he condemned sin in sinful man, in order that the righteous _____ (16) of the law might be fully met in us, who do not live according to the sinful nature but according to the Spirit.*

I believe that working for financial gain or causing someone else to work is wrong.

When we go out to eat, we are causing our men and our maidservants to work. We call them _____ (17), waitresses, and store clerks. What would happen if the Christians stopped shopping and eating out on Sunday?

 If God is going to heal our land, we must turn back to His laws and stop desecrating the Sabbath.

If we want to see God heal our land, then we must turn from our _____ (18) ways. If we want to continue to go into slavery and lose all of the freedoms that we now hold so dear, let's just keep following the world and eating out on Sunday.

If you work in an_____ (19) field—medical, fire, police—a position that requires round-the-clock supervision, then God has made the exception for you to work. If you are able to have Sundays off, then you should honor the Sabbath.

When we first committed to again honoring the Sabbath, we ran out of _____ (20) on Sunday. You will only have to do that a few times until you remember to plan ahead.

Plan ahead. Buy gas earlier, buy milk, get enough groceries; let's no longer honor the blue law, but let's again honor God's law on this topic. Let's live as if the blue law never changed and let's not _____ (21) anything on the Sabbath.

 Can you wash clothes or dishes? Can you work in the garden? Can you clean house? Can you change the oil? Can you wash the car?

All of these are good questions and they should be taken to the Lord for your answer. If you are doing something that is strenuous or _____ (22), then it probably should wait.

Remember that *the Sabbath was made for man (Mark 2:27)*. It is a day of
_____ (23) and relaxation from the hectic work week.
It is a day to spend with the Lord, your family, and your church family.

Satan's goal is to get us to _____ (24) God's
commands—from getting us to desecrate the Sabbath, to getting us to
accept immoralities into our lives. His goal is to defeat us and destroy
our children.

BLESSINGS FOLLOW REPENTANCE

**You say that you believe in the_____ (25), but do
they see you read it or take it to your place of employment?**

**You say that you believe sexual immorality is
_____ (26), but do you support it in what you are
watching?**

**You say that cursing is wrong, but do you allow it into your
_____ (27) by way of the TV?**

**Will you be the church that repents? Will you begin the
revival?**

The church of today needs missionaries to lead in this repentance. It
needs people to begin to speak up for God and His Word. God wants
you to be His witness in our morally decaying church.

YOU WILL BE PERSECUTED FOR YOUR STANCE

> *Matthew 5:10–12: Blessed are those who are persecuted
> because of _____ (28), for theirs is
> the kingdom of heaven. Blessed are you when people insult you,
> persecute you and falsely say all kinds of evil against you
> because of me. Rejoice and be glad, because great is your
> reward in heaven, for in the same way they persecuted the*

prophets who were before you.

Let's begin to make our country wonder what is going on with the
_____ (29). They no longer support immoral
movies, they no longer desecrate the Sabbath, and they are making
prayer and God's Word a priority in their lives.

HONOR THE SABBATH

I commit that I will no longer miss church for work, for things of this
world, for entertainment, for laziness, or for selfish reasons. I will no
longer honor the changing of the blue law, but I will honor God's Law. I
realize that I reap what I sow. I am ready to stand up for Jesus and His
Word and to call the church back to Him. (Isaiah 56:2; 58:13,14; 1 John
2:15–17; James 4:4; Leviticus 19:1–3; Exodus 20: 8–11; 31:13–17; Acts
20:7; Revelation 1:10)

BEFORE LESSON 4 READ THROUGH:

COMMITMENT THREE   *67*

COMMITMENT 3
HONOR THE SABBATH

THE THIRD COMMITMENT:
HONOR THE SABBATH

I commit that I will no longer miss church for work, for things of this world, for entertainment, for laziness, or for selfish reasons. I will no longer honor the changing of the blue law, but I will honor God's Law. I realize that I reap what I sow. I am ready to stand up for Jesus and His Word and to call the church back to Him. (Isaiah 56:2; 58:13,14; 1 John 2:15–17; James 4:4; Leviticus 19:1–3; Exodus 20: 8–11; 31:13–17; Acts 20:7; Revelation 1:10)

A few years ago *USA Today* came out with an article that said, "Young adults aren't sticking with church, 70 percent of surveyed Protestants stopped attending by age 23." Today the statistics are even higher. The Barna group wrote a book a few years ago called *unChristian*, which found that Christians in their 20s did not believe that a person's faith in God is meant to be developed in a local church.

* 88 percent of students from "Christian" homes deny their faith before they graduate from college.
* 91 percent of students from evangelical churches do not believe in absolute moral truth (http://codebluerally.com/info.php).

The statistics should alarm us. What are we doing wrong? We have already talked about the deception of Satan and his influence on our lives through the media, but now we will move into our actions on the Sabbath.

> *Exodus 20:8–11: Remember the Sabbath day by keeping it holy. Six days you shall labor and do all your work, but the seventh day is a Sabbath to the LORD your God. On it you shall not do any work, neither you, nor your son or daughter, nor your manservant or maidservant, nor your animals, nor the alien within your gates. For in six days the LORD made the heavens and the earth, the sea, and all that is in them, but he rested on*

the seventh day. Therefore the LORD blessed the Sabbath day and made it holy.

Exodus 31:12–17: Then the LORD said to Moses, "Say to the Israelites, 'You must observe my Sabbaths. This will be a sign between me and you for the generations to come, so you may know that I am the LORD, who makes you holy. Observe the Sabbath, because it is holy to you. Anyone who desecrates it must be put to death; whoever does any work on that day must be cut off from his people. For six days, work is to be done, but the seventh day is a Sabbath of rest, holy to the LORD. Whoever does any work on the Sabbath day must be put to death. The Israelites are to observe the Sabbath, celebrating it for the generations to come as a lasting covenant. It will be a sign between me and the Israelites forever, for in six days the LORD made the heavens and the earth, and on the seventh day he abstained from work and rested.'"

FROM SATURDAY TO SUNDAY

The seventh day that God rested on was Saturday, but after the Lord was resurrected on Sunday, the church began to honor the Sabbath on Sunday, the first day of the week. This became known as the Lord's Day. I love how Matthew Henry puts it in his commentary when he speaks of the Old Testament Sabbath on Saturday as being a shadow of the New Testament Sabbath, which is now held on the day Christ arose, Sunday.

Acts 20:7: On the first day of the week we came together to break bread. Paul spoke to the people and, because he intended to leave the next day, kept on talking until midnight.

Revelation 1:10: On the Lord's Day I was in the Spirit, and I heard behind me a loud voice like a trumpet.

When our country was founded upon God's principles and laws we continued to honor the Lord's Day and we took seriously the Scriptures about the Sabbath. Today, we are desecrating the Lord's Day.

Why does our country vote on Tuesday? One of the reasons we vote on Tuesday is because when voting began, people had to travel far distances to get to the polling booths. If they would have voted on Monday, many Christians would have missed the vote because they would not have left on a Sunday to make it to the booth on Monday. Generations of the past took honoring the Sabbath very seriously. It was a day of rest for the family. It was a day to get together with your local church. Families of today are falling apart, and I believe that one of the main reasons is that we are so distant from one another. We rush from one thing to another. We are disconnected from the members of our own family. The Sabbath was made for us and it is a blessing for us. What if families stopped rushing around on Sunday and actually spent some time together?

PUTTING GOD FIRST IN OUR LIVES

The Bible says in Exodus chapter 20 that the Sabbath is a day that will show the generations to come that we are God's people and that it is He that makes us holy. We show the world that it is He that makes us holy and we show our dependence upon Him by how we honor the Sabbath.

Many Christians would respond that God is first in their lives, but their actions may be saying something different. For example, let's say that you are a member of a church and that you attend church most of the time, but there are some Sundays that you miss. You miss for hunting, vacation, professional sporting events (live or on TV), your child's practice or game, a concert, a movie, a television show, or just because you feel like staying home.

When we miss church for selfish reasons, aren't we telling the world that God is first in our lives unless something better comes along? How many people sit bored in church on Sunday and then cheer at their favorite sporting event? What are we showing God? What are we teaching our children? Shouldn't we be excited to come and worship the God who created and died for us? Shouldn't we be saying no to the temptations of this world and yes to God?

> *Isaiah 58:13–14: "If you keep your feet from breaking the Sabbath and from doing as you please on my holy day, if you call the Sabbath a delight and the LORD'S holy day honorable, and if you honor it by not going your own way and not doing as you please or speaking idle words, then you will find your joy in the LORD, and I will cause you to ride on the heights of the land and to feast on the inheritance of your father Jacob." The mouth of the LORD has spoken.*

> *Isaiah 56:2: Blessed is the man who does this, the man who holds it fast, who keeps the Sabbath without desecrating it, and keeps his hand from doing any evil.*

SOWING SEEDS OF DOUBT

Have you ever arrived at church and wondered where your friends are? You anticipated talking to them and sharing news of events from your week. You longed to see them and be encouraged by them, but where were they? Why weren't they there? When you found out where they were how did you feel? If they missed because of sickness or another "acceptable" reason you most likely felt compassion, but if they missed church for selfish reasons, you were most likely disappointed and discouraged, maybe even irritated. If they went to a ball game or just stayed home to watch TV instead of coming to worship with you, it might have caused you to feel a little rejected. They sowed a seed of doubt within you. Have you ever missed church for selfish reasons? Do you sow seeds of doubt into other believers? When you miss for selfish reasons, then it justifies them in missing as well, and a vicious cycle begins. What would Jesus be doing? Would He be at the Super Bowl, or would He be in church worshiping and serving others?

IT IS NO COINCIDENCE

Satan has a goal and he knows how to achieve his purposes. He is very crafty. He knew that when television came out, he could not show the things that are on today all at once. He desensitized us a little at a time. He has done the same with the Sabbath.

THE BLUE LAW

The blue law is a type of law typically found in the United States and designed to enforce moral standards, particularly the observance of Sunday as a day of worship or rest, and restrict Sunday shopping.

In America the law was changed in the 1980s. At first it stated that businesses will only be open during non-church hours and no alcohol will be sold. Today almost everything can be open and alcohol can be sold. Sunday is now the second-busiest shopping day of the week. Perhaps Christians eating out for Sunday lunch have had a lot to do with this.

Can you see the progression of evil? Is it a coincidence that the Super Bowl and many other tempting events are now held on Sunday? Did you know that graduation ceremonies are headed in this direction? How many Christians miss church because they have season tickets to a sporting team? How many Christians miss church because they get tickets to a concert? How many Christians go boating or to the lake many weekends in a row and miss church? Where will it end? What is the standard we are to live by?

Even though the world turns against God's law, is it right for His people to follow them? Shouldn't we be setting the example as to what should be done on the Sabbath? Even though man's law says it's okay, is that enough to break God's law? Who is leading whom?

THE RETURN OF GOD'S POWER

Are you sick and tired of being ridiculed for your faith? Are you tired of the media cutting us down and saying that we are narrow minded? Then repent and allow God to glorify Himself through you! Turn back to the principles that our country was founded upon and watch God do some amazing things. The church I pastor has begun to take these commitments seriously, and we are seeing God do some amazing things in and through us. If the church would get rid of our idols, make prayer and God's Word a priority, and recommit to honoring the Sabbath, God might heal our land. Do you want to see the lost saved? Do you want to see the laws and our leaders following God's Word? Then, we must repent.

HOW TO DEFINE WORK

> **Exodus 20:9–10:** *Six days you shall labor and do all your work, but the seventh day is a Sabbath to the LORD your God. On it you shall not do any work, neither you, nor your son or daughter, nor your manservant or maidservant, nor your animals, nor the alien within your gates.*

In the Interbiblical period the Sabbath became the heart of the law, and the prohibitions were expanded. Thirty-nine tasks were banned, such as tying or untying a knot. In the New Testament the habit of Jesus was to observe the Sabbath as a day of worship in the synagogues (Luke 4:16), but His failure to comply with the minute restrictions brought conflict (Mark 2:23–28; 3:1–6; Luke 13:10–17; John 5:1–18). (*Holman Bible Dictionary*)

What can we do and not do on the Sabbath?

I believe that missing church for anything other than an emergency or sickness is wrong. In Acts, people missed church because of (vacations) mission trips, but they worshiped with other believers on the Sabbath. If we go out of town, we should still make it a priority to worship with other Christians on the Sabbath (Matthew 12:11, 12).

Over the years I have met many individuals who say that they are Christians and yet they do not attend church. Their argument is always the same, "You do not have to go to church to be saved." This statement is true, but it is not the entire picture. You do not have to attend church to be saved, but attending church is evidence of your salvation. It is evidence that Christ is in you, empowering you to obey His ways. We are called to be Christlike. Would Christ attend church? Would He love others and forgive them when they offended Him, or would He stay home and sulk and hold a grudge and say, "You do not have to attend church to be saved."

> **Hebrews 10:25:** *Let us not give up meeting together, as some are in the habit of doing, but let us encourage one another— and all the more as you see the Day approaching.*

> **Romans 8:3–4:** *For what the law was powerless to do in that it was weakened by the sinful nature, God did by sending his own Son in the likeness of sinful man to be a sin offering. And so he condemned sin in sinful man, in order that the righteous requirements of the law might be fully met in us, who do not live according to the sinful nature but according to the Spirit.*

I believe that working for financial gain or causing someone else to work is wrong. The Scriptures clearly tell us to not to work on the Sabbath or to cause anyone else to work as well. When we go out to eat, we are causing our men and our maidservants to work. We call them waiters, waitresses, and store clerks. What would happen if the Christians stopped shopping and eating out on Sunday? Most likely, many restaurants would close and their employees would have an opportunity to worship God. The world would wonder what is going on, and they would persecute us, but we are not looking for praise from them, we are looking to praise our God. We are seeking to show them a sign of who is important to us. If God is going to heal our land, we must turn back to His laws and stop desecrating the Sabbath.

What about Christian athletes that play on Sunday? Since I live in St. Louis, I am a huge fan of Kurt Warner and Albert Pujols. I enjoy watching them and seeing them succeed. I love to watch them give God the glory for their success. But do their success or their actions dictate what is right or moral? No. God's Word reveals to us what is right and moral. What about Eric Liddell, who refused to run in the Olympics because his race was scheduled on a Sunday? Where are the men and women of the faith who will stand up and say, "No, I cannot work on Sunday"? Perhaps if more Christians stopped eating out and shopping on the Sabbath our country would again return to its roots of honoring the Sabbath. By the way, the Super Bowl and baseball games were not always played on Sundays. There has been a gradual decline in the moral decay of our society. It is time for us to wake up and return to God's laws. Satan is not going to tempt us with boring temptations. He is going to pull out all the stops and appeal to our flesh that will desire to do wrong. Sin is pleasing for a moment, but godliness is forever. What will we continue to choose? If we want to see God heal our land, then we must turn from our wicked ways. If we want to continue to go into slavery and lose all of the freedoms that we now hold so dear, let's just keep following the world and eating out on Sunday.

What about Christians whose bosses require them to work on Sunday? Unless they work in the emergency field, they should begin seeking to be off on the Sabbath. I would encourage them to pray and ask the Lord for forgiveness in this area and then to go into their boss's office and ask if they could have off on Sunday to worship Jesus their God. Ask the Lord to go with you and to give you favor. We need to begin to stand up for His laws once again and speak out for our beliefs in this matter. No longer should we just accept the fact that we work on Sunday. If their boss refuses to allow them off on Sunday, then they should actively pursue another profession. A person might say, "But what about my benefits?" To them I would respond, "Which benefits? Your earthly benefits or your heavenly benefits?" God does not always ask us to do easy things. Sometimes He asks us to do hard things like take our son up a mountain to sacrifice him or to hide in caves even though we know we are the anointed king or to be a slave and prisoner even though we know the dream He gave us. It is not always easy to pick up our cross and follow Him. In fact, He might ask us to sell all that we have and follow Him. God is the one who provides for us and we can trust Him. There is also the responsibility of the church in this area. If a member loses a job because of standing up for God's law in this area, then the church has a responsibility to support that brother or sister until they can find other employment. This is the church being the church. Yes, people might have to sell land or other valuables to support others, but isn't this the picture we have of the church in Acts? They were not so much concerned about their possessions on this earth as entering into their heavenly home.

If you work in an emergency field—medical, fire, police—a position that requires round-the-clock supervision, then God has made the exception for you to work. If you are able to have Sundays off, then you should honor the Sabbath.

What if your boss allowed you to have off on Sunday, but he forced you to do more work during the week, because of your commitment? Would this make working on Sunday all right? Doesn't Peter teach us that we are to suffer for doing what is right, and to this we are called? Will God not bless him for his obedience and curse him for his disobedience?

A man informed me that he is all for not eating out on Sunday, but that is going to cause his wife to do something she does not like to do on the Sabbath, cook. She enjoys getting a break on Sunday from cooking and cleaning and she likes to go out to eat. My wife does not like to cook very much on Sunday, either, and so we plan ahead. We have leftovers or we purchase a sub sandwich earlier in the week. You could buy frozen lasagna or something similar; it just takes some planning and dedication to God on the issue. When we first committed to honor the Sabbath, we ran out of milk on Sunday. You will only have to do that a few times until you remember to plan ahead.

When we began this commitment with our church, there came a Sunday that we were combining with another church for a joint fellowship meal and a service together. Early Sunday morning my wife arose and began to rethink all of the details. She began to wonder if we were going to have enough food for everyone. She began to fret and wonder if she should go to the store early Sunday morning to get just a few more things. As she worried, she decided that she would just trust God and see what happens. Guess what? We had twelve basketfuls left over.

Plan ahead. Buy gas earlier, buy milk, get enough groceries; let's no longer honor the changing of the blue law, but let's again honor God's law on this topic. Let's live as if the blue law never changed and let's not purchase anything on the Sabbath. Our forefathers kept this day holy and so should we. Let's stop holding conferences, attending concerts, and using the transportation avenues on Sunday. Do we really need to fly off on Sunday to be at our meeting, or could we rearrange the schedule just a little to honor God on His holy day?

If there is an emergency, then Jesus would approve of you helping another, but be careful as to what you call an emergency. Sometimes, we make it into an emergency, but it really could wait or it is our procrastination that caused it to be an emergency. Remember that God is the one who blesses our obedience and He judges the motives of our heart.

Can you wash clothes or dishes? Can you work in the garden? Can you clean house? Can you change the oil? Can you wash the car?

All of these are good questions and they should be taken to the Lord for your answer. If you are doing something that is strenuous or stressful, then it probably should wait. Remember that *the Sabbath was made for man (Mark 2:27)*. It is a day of rest and relaxation from the hectic work week. It is a day to spend with the Lord, your family, and your church family.

Each one of us has to make some tough decisions. We must reevaluate our lives. What are we living for? We must put Christ first in our lives and not allow the fleshly desires to cause us to disobey His Word. Satan's goal is to get us to break God's commands—from getting us to desecrate the Sabbath, to getting us to accept immoralities into our lives. His goal is to defeat us and destroy our children. He is winning. We must repent! Repentance is hard—it is self-denial, it is picking up one's cross, and it is laying down our lives to please Jesus in every area. The benefits are out of this world! He doesn't want any robots in heaven. He is looking for people who will choose Him over all of this life's desires. For us to be able to obey, we must have the Holy Spirit enabling us. We must seek God's strength and wisdom in these areas. We must ask Him to forgive us for our disobedience and then to empower us to have the boldness to ask off and tell others that we will no longer desecrate the Sabbath.

But pastors work on Sunday! This argument seemed silly to me, but it made me reevaluate what I do and do not do on Sunday. God gets to set the rules and He desires that church be done in a fitting and orderly manner. The Scriptures teach that at church certain things need to go on for our services. Since He sets the rules then, it is okay for a pastor to fulfill his Sunday duties, and other such ministers and servants. It is an honor to serve the Lord in worship and not a strenuous activity. The question made me think about what I should do as a pastor on Sunday. I no longer write newsletters or do other ministerial work on Sunday except going over my sermon and other such activities for that day's worship service.

BLESSINGS FOLLOW REPENTANCE

Since our church has committed to these five commitments, we have seen God do some wonderful things. A gentleman in our church is an avid fisherman who goes on many fishing tournaments. When the commitment to honor the Sabbath came up, he had to make some tough decisions, because the tournaments usually end on Sunday afternoons. He decided to make it a point to leave the tournaments early and come and worship with his family. As the commitment grew in their house, this couple decided that they did not need to shop any longer on the Sabbath, as well. Since that commitment, their daughter who is a freshman in college is not wavering in if she should follow the Lord or not. She is excelling in her relationship with Christ and she is one of our youth leaders. Their son, who is a junior in college and has been struggling with spiritual issues, has gotten saved and is reading God's Word daily. He even carries his Bible to classes on a secular campus. Would your son or daughter be doing that? If not, perhaps they need to see you make some tough decisions about your faith. You say that you believe in the Bible, but do they see you read it or take it to your place of employment? You say that you believe sexual immorality is wrong, but do you support it in what you are watching? You say that cursing is wrong, but do you allow it into your home by way of the TV? You say that God is first in your life, but do you miss church whenever something better comes along? Will you stand up for Christ and His ways and teach your children how to abstain from immoralities?

Another lady in our church went to apply for a part-time job, and the manager informed her that everyone has to work on Sunday. She was debating about just accepting this as fact or standing up for her new commitment. When she went in for the final interview, she informed the manager that she would not be able to come in on Sunday because of her commitment. God then showed her favor. The manager said that they would like to hire her anyway and she would not have to work on Sunday. It may not work out this way every time. You may have to go on a few interviews, but God is faithful and He will take care of us.

Will you be the church that repents? Will you begin the revival?

The church of today needs missionaries to lead in this repentance. It needs people to begin to speak up for God and His Word. God wants you to be His witness in our morally decaying church.

YOU WILL BE PERSECUTED FOR YOUR STANCE

> *Matthew 5:10–12:* *Blessed are those who are persecuted because of righteousness, for theirs is the kingdom of heaven. Blessed are you when people insult you, persecute you and falsely say all kinds of evil against you because of me. Rejoice and be glad, because great is your reward in heaven, for in the same way they persecuted the prophets who were before you.*

You will be persecuted if you begin to stand up for God's morals in your media choices. You will be persecuted if you stand up and begin to honor the Sabbath. Some of the persecutions will come from your family, friends, the church, and your flesh. Are you ready? Are you willing? Do you see the decay in our country?

Let's begin to make our country wonder what is going on with the Christians. They no longer support immoral movies, they no longer desecrate the Sabbath, and they are making prayer and God's Word a priority in their lives. What next? Keep reading.

HONOR THE SABBATH

I commit that I will no longer miss church for work, for things of this world, for entertainment, for laziness, or for selfish reasons. I will no longer honor the changing of the blue law, but I will honor God's Law. I realize that I reap what I sow. I am ready to stand up for Jesus and His Word and to call the church back to Him. (Isaiah 56:2; 58:13,14; 1 John 2:15–17; James 4:4; Leviticus 19:1–3; Exodus 20: 8–11; 31:13–17; Acts 20:7; Revelation 1:10)

LESSON FOUR
BRING IN THE TITHES AND OFFERINGS

HOW MUCH ARE WE TO GIVE BACK TO GOD?

> ***2 Corinthians 9:6–7:*** *Remember this: Whoever sows sparingly will also reap sparingly, and whoever sows generously will also reap generously. Each man should give what he has decided in his heart to give, not reluctantly or under compulsion, for God loves a _____ (1) giver.*

Many Christians interpret this verse to mean that Christians are no longer bound to give ten percent of their income, which is called a tithe, but Paul is talking to them about an_____ (2) not their tithe. Look at the context of this verse.

> ***2 Corinthians 8:13–14:*** *Our desire is not that others might be relieved while you are hard pressed, but that there might be equality. At the present time your plenty will supply what _____ (3) need, so that in turn their plenty will supply what you need. Then there will be equality.*

Paul is asking them to collect an offering to help out other Christians in need. Look at this next verse.

> ***2 Corinthians 8:19:*** *What is more, he was chosen by the churches to accompany us as we carry the _____ (4), which we administer in order to honor the Lord himself and to show our eagerness to help.*

The _____ (5) is ten percent of whatever the Lord blesses you with, right off of the top.

An_____ (6) is a gift for which you can decide what amount to give.

DID JESUS EVER SPEAK ABOUT TITHING?

Matthew 23:23: Woe to you, teachers of the law and Pharisees, you hypocrites! You give a _____ (7) of your spices—mint, dill and cummin. But you have neglected the more important matters of the law—justice, mercy and faithfulness. You should have practiced the latter, without neglecting the former.

But notice that Jesus did not say you need to be more loving to others and forget about the tithe.

TITHES AND OFFERINGS

Malachi gives us the clearest warning upon the matter of God's people not bringing in the tithes and offerings.

Malachi 3:6–18: "I the LORD do not change. So you, O descendants of Jacob, are not destroyed. Ever since the time of your forefathers you have turned away from my decrees and have not kept them. Return to me, and I will return to you," says the LORD Almighty. "But you ask, 'How are we to return?' Will a man rob God? Yet you rob me. But you ask, 'How do we rob you?' In_____ (8) and _____ (9). You are under a _____ (10)—the whole nation of you—because you are robbing me. Bring the _____ (11) tithe into the storehouse, that there may be food in my house. Test me in this," says the LORD Almighty, "and see if I will not throw open the floodgates of heaven and pour out so much blessing that you will not have room enough for it. I will prevent pests from devouring your crops, and the vines in your fields will not cast their fruit," says the LORD Almighty. "Then all the nations *will call you _____ (12), for yours will be a delightful land," says the LORD Almighty. "You have said harsh things against me," says the LORD. "Yet you ask, 'What have we said against you?' You have said, 'It is futile to serve God. What did we gain by carrying out his requirements and going about like mourners before the LORD Almighty? But now we call the arrogant blessed. Certainly the evildoers prosper, and even those who challenge God escape.'" Then those who feared the LORD talked with each other, and the LORD listened and heard. A scroll of remembrance was written in his presence concerning those who feared the LORD and honored his name. "They will be mine," says the LORD Almighty, "in the day when I make up my treasured possession. I will spare them, just as in compassion a man spares his son who serves him. And you will again see the distinction between the righteous and the wicked, between those who serve God and those who do not."*

Give the _____ (13) ten percent to God and then figure out the rest of your bills. Put God first in your life.

What are we showing God that we love the most when we choose to spend our money on selfish things instead of bringing in the 10 percent that He requires? Are we thankful for the prosperity of our country?

Perhaps if we are not tithing God is going to take more than ten percent in the _____ (14). The cursing could come in many forms: your income, things constantly breaking down, and other such financial difficulties.

DOES OUR ECONOMY HAVE ANYTHING TO DO WITH OUR OBEDIENCE IN THIS AREA?

Look at what the Lord promises for His obedient people.

> **Deuteronomy 28:9–14:** *The LORD will establish you as his holy people, as he promised you on oath, if you keep the commands of the LORD your God and walk in his ways. Then all the peoples on earth will see that you are called by the name of the LORD, and they will fear you. The LORD will grant you _____ (15) prosperity—in the fruit of your womb, the young of your livestock and the crops of your ground—in the land he swore to your forefathers to give you. The LORD will open the heavens, the storehouse of his bounty, to send rain on your land in season and to bless all the work of your hands. You will lend to many nations but will _____ (16) from none. The LORD will make you the head, not the tail. If you pay attention to the commands of the LORD your God that I give you this day and _____ (17) follow them, you will always be at the top, never at the bottom. Do not turn aside from any of the commands I give you today, to the right or to the left, following other gods and serving them.*

Have we not had abundant prosperity in the past? Did we not lend to many nations in the past? The Lord blesses us for obedience and He curses for our disobedience. Look at this curse from Scripture.

> **Deuteronomy 28:43–48:** *The alien who lives among you will rise above you higher and higher, but you will sink lower and lower. He will _____ (18) to you, but you will not lend to him. He will be the head, but you will be the tail. All these curses will come upon you. They will pursue you and overtake you until you are destroyed, because you did not obey the LORD your God and observe the commands and decrees he gave you. They will be a sign and a wonder to you and your*

*descendants forever. Because you did not serve the LORD your
God joyfully and gladly in the time of* _____
*(19), therefore in hunger and thirst, in nakedness and dire
poverty, you will serve the enemies the LORD sends against you.
He will put an iron yoke on your neck until he has destroyed
you.*

America is no longer the lender and we have and are creating a
tremendous debt.

Unless we repent, unless we figure out how we are disobeying God, we
will continue to go into slavery and our enemies will overtake us.

Tithes and offerings have been around since Genesis. Abraham gave a
tenth to Melchizedek, and Cain and Abel brought offerings to the Lord
(Genesis 14:18; 4:1–4).

> **Deuteronomy 14:22:** *Be sure to set* _____ *(20)
> a tenth of all that your fields produce each year.*

> **Leviticus 27:30:** *A tithe of everything from the land, whether
> grain from the soil or fruit from the trees, belongs to the LORD;
> it is* _____ *(21) to the LORD.*

What if God's people took seriously that the ten percent that God
requires is holy?

Let's turn back to the One who can turn all things around and make
our silver and gold _____ (22).

Give to God _____ (23) and then watch what He will
do.

BRING IN THE TITHES AND OFFERINGS

I will not rob God. I will bring in the whole tithe and offering. I will do this cheerfully because I love and trust God for all of my blessings. I also realize that our nation is under a curse because of our unfaithfulness in this area. (2 Corinthians 8:19; 9:6–7; Malachi 3:6–18; Matthew 23:23)

BEFORE LESSON 5 READ THROUGH:

COMMITMENT FOUR   *87*

COMMITMENT 4

BRING IN THE TITHES AND OFFERINGS

THE FOURTH COMMITMENT:
BRING IN THE TITHES AND OFFERINGS

I will not rob God. I will bring in the whole tithe and offering. I will do this cheerfully because I love and trust God for all of my blessings. I also realize that our nation is under a curse because of our unfaithfulness in this area. (2 Corinthians 8:19; 9:6–7; Malachi 3:6–18; Matthew 23:23)

HOW MUCH ARE WE TO GIVE BACK TO GOD?

> *2 Corinthians 9:6–7: Remember this: Whoever sows sparingly will also reap sparingly, and whoever sows generously will also reap generously. Each man should give what he has decided in his heart to give, not reluctantly or under compulsion, for God loves a cheerful giver.*

Many Christians interpret this verse to mean that Christians are no longer bound to give ten percent of their income, which is called a tithe, but Paul is talking to them about an offering not their tithe. Look at the context of this verse.

> *2 Corinthians 8:13–14: Our desire is not that others might be relieved while you are hard pressed, but that there might be equality. At the present time your plenty will supply what they need, so that in turn their plenty will supply what you need. Then there will be equality.*

Paul is asking them to collect an offering to help out other Christians in need. Look at this next verse.

> *2 Corinthians 8:19: What is more, he was chosen by the churches to accompany us as we carry the offering, which we administer in order to honor the Lord himself and to show our eagerness to help.*

The tithe is ten percent of whatever the Lord blesses you with, right off of the top. It is to be set aside first and not given as a leftover after you pay your bills. An offering is a gift for which you can decide what amount to give. If you give an offering sparingly you will reap sparingly, but if you give generously you will reap generously. You should not give an offering reluctantly or under compulsion, for "God loves a cheerful giver" (2 Corinthians 9:7).

DID JESUS EVER SPEAK ABOUT TITHING?

> *Matthew 23:23:* *Woe to you, teachers of the law and Pharisees, you hypocrites! You give a tenth of your spices—mint, dill and cummin. But you have neglected the more important matters of the law—justice, mercy and faithfulness. You should have practiced the latter, without neglecting the former.*

Jesus was upset with the Pharisees because they were tithing their spice racks, but they were forgetting to show people justice, mercy, and faithfulness. They were proud and showy of their works for God, and they were unconcerned about the matter of loving their neighbor as themselves. They were more concerned with how men perceived them than about how God perceives them. But notice that Jesus did not say you need to be more loving to others and forget about the tithe. No, Jesus said you should be tithing even to your spice rack without neglecting to show justice, mercy, and faithfulness.

TITHES AND OFFERINGS

Malachi gives us the clearest warning upon the matter of God's people not bringing in the tithes and offerings.

> *Malachi 3:6–18:* *"I the LORD do not change. So you, O descendants of Jacob, are not destroyed. Ever since the time of your forefathers you have turned away from my decrees and have not kept them. Return to me, and I will return to you,"* says the LORD Almighty. *"But you ask, 'How are we to return?' Will a man rob God? Yet you rob me. But you ask, 'How do we rob you?' In tithes and offerings. You are under a curse—the*

whole nation of you—because you are robbing me. Bring the whole tithe into the storehouse, that there may be food in my house. Test me in this," says the LORD Almighty, "and see if I will not throw open the floodgates of heaven and pour out so much blessing that you will not have room enough for it. I will prevent pests from devouring your crops, and the vines in your fields will not cast their fruit," says the LORD Almighty. "Then all the nations will call you blessed, for yours will be a delightful land," says the LORD Almighty. "You have said harsh things against me," says the LORD. "Yet you ask, 'What have we said against you?' You have said, 'It is futile to serve God. What did we gain by carrying out his requirements and going about like mourners before the LORD Almighty? But now we call the arrogant blessed. Certainly the evildoers prosper, and even those who challenge God escape.'" Then those who feared the LORD talked with each other, and the LORD listened and heard. A scroll of remembrance was written in his presence concerning those who feared the LORD and honored his name. "They will be mine," says the LORD Almighty, "in the day when I make up my treasured possession. I will spare them, just as in compassion a man spares his son who serves him. And you will again see the distinction between the righteous and the wicked, between those who serve God and those who do not."

A tithe is ten percent of what the Lord provides for you. An offering is something over and above the tithe. The tithe goes into the storehouse (church) to provide for the needs of the body and to minister to needs in the community and further the gospel. An offering is taken to meet special needs like the one for the Macedonian churches in 2 Corinthians. If your church takes an offering to meet a need, you are not supposed to give your tithe to meet that need. You should give your tithe to the Lord, through your local church, and then decide what offering you are to give to meet that need. Church treasurers can see that we rob God in our tithes when offerings are taken. Do we think that God does not notice? Do we not reap what we sow?

In verse fifteen it tells us that when we begin to become selfish and hold our money in a tight fist, we will call the arrogant blessed. Are we calling the arrogant blessed? Do we long to be a Hollywood movie star? Do our children long to be the next star on *American Idol?* Do we watch with anticipation the next person on *Deal or no Deal,* hoping that they will get what we dream of—riches and fame? What are we longing for—the desire to be rich? How many Christians do not pay their tithes and offerings, but buy Powerball tickets and go to the casino? We call the rich and famous blessed and we say that it is futile to bring in our tithes and offerings.

I used to counsel people to start giving something to God. Start with two percent and then work your way up to ten percent. I no longer counsel people in this way. Now I say, first give the whole ten percent to God and then figure out the rest of your bills. Put God first in your life.

I have heard the argument that God would not want me to have a bad credit rating, and in order for me to pay my bills I have to cut back on the tithe. What credit rating should we be concerned about? Shouldn't we be more concerned about our credit rating with God than the world's? In most budget counseling you will find many things that the counselee is considering a necessity that is not. For example, do you really need to have cable or satellite TV? Do you really need a cell phone with all of the bells and whistles? Do you really need to be eating out so much? Do you really need such a large house and fancy cars? Perhaps we should live within the means He has provided for us and not the means the world says we should have. What are we showing God that we love the most when we choose to spend our money on selfish things instead of bringing in the 10 percent that He requires? Are we thankful for the prosperity of our country? We should be glad that He requires only 10 percent instead of 90 percent! God does want you to have a good credit rating with the world and to pay them what you owe, but He also wants you to be content with what you have and to not live beyond your means.

It is amazing to me how many faithful families bring in their tithes and seem to struggle less. Perhaps if we are not tithing God is going to take more than ten percent in the cursing. The cursing could come in many forms: your income, things constantly breaking down, and other such financial difficulties. Remember that it was in the desert that His people wandered for forty years and yet, their shoes and clothes did not wear out. God can bless our obedience and He will curse our disobedience.

Your checkbook will reveal a lot about you and what you love. What does your checkbook reveal about your love for God?

Should I tithe on the net or on the gross? I guess that depends upon which you would like to be blessed upon. Do you want to be blessed upon the net or the gross? If we are to pay God first, then it would make sense to me that we should pay Him even before we pay our taxes.

DOES OUR ECONOMY HAVE ANYTHING TO DO WITH OUR OBEDIENCE IN THIS AREA?

Look at what the Lord promises for His obedient people.

> ***Deuteronomy 28:9–14:*** *The LORD will establish you as his holy people, as he promised you on oath, if you keep the commands of the LORD your God and walk in his ways. Then all the peoples on earth will see that you are called by the name of the LORD, and they will fear you. The LORD will grant you abundant prosperity—in the fruit of your womb, the young of your livestock and the crops of your ground—in the land he swore to your forefathers to give you. The LORD will open the heavens, the storehouse of his bounty, to send rain on your land in season and to bless all the work of your hands. You will lend to many nations but will borrow from none. The LORD will make you the head, not the tail. If you pay attention to the commands of the LORD your God that I give you this day and carefully*

follow them, you will always be at the top, never at the bottom.
Do not turn aside from any of the commands I give you today,
to the right or to the left, following other gods and serving them.

Have we not had abundant prosperity in the past? Did we not lend to many nations in the past? The Lord blesses us for obedience and He curses for our disobedience. Look at this curse from Scripture.

> **Deuteronomy 28:43–48:** *The alien who lives among you will rise above you higher and higher, but you will sink lower and lower. He will lend to you, but you will not lend to him. He will be the head, but you will be the tail. All these curses will come upon you. They will pursue you and overtake you until you are destroyed, because you did not obey the LORD your God and observe the commands and decrees he gave you. They will be a sign and a wonder to you and your descendants forever. Because you did not serve the LORD your God joyfully and gladly in the time of prosperity, therefore in hunger and thirst, in nakedness and dire poverty, you will serve the enemies the LORD sends against you. He will put an iron yoke on your neck until he has destroyed you.*

America is no longer the lender and we have and are creating a tremendous debt. We are no longer the head and we are becoming the tail. Unless we repent, unless we figure out how we are disobeying God, we will continue to go into slavery and our enemies will overtake us. The Bible warns us that when we prosper, we must hold fast to the ways of God and worship God joyfully, gladly, and bring in the tithes and offerings. Let me ask you a question. Do you long to go to church and worship God, or would you rather go to a sporting event or go shopping at the mall? Have we forgotten who has blessed our nation and whom we are to serve joyfully and gladly? Would you rather be somewhere else on Sunday? Is going to church a burden to you? For some, going to church is not a burden, but for many it is. We must repent.

Tithes and offerings have been around since Genesis. Abraham gave a tenth to Melchizedek, and Cain and Abel brought offerings to the Lord (Genesis 14:18; 4:1–4). It is something that we can do to show God that we are thankful and grateful for all of His many blessings. It is an attitude of our heart. Do we love and trust Him? Do we believe that He can control the economy and the fruits of our hands?

> **Deuteronomy 14:22:** *Be sure to set aside a tenth of all that your fields produce each year.*

> **Leviticus 27:30:** *A tithe of everything from the land, whether grain from the soil or fruit from the trees, belongs to the LORD; it is holy to the LORD.*

What if God's people took seriously that the ten percent that God requires is holy? What if we began to bring in the tithes and offerings? Perhaps God would throw open the flood gates of heaven. Dr. Dobson could be our spokesman. He could go to the president, hand him a check, and say, "Mr. President, the Christians would like to pay off the national debt." Could you imagine? Could God do it? Let me tell you about a tremendous blessing on a smaller scale.

Our church has begun to take these commitments seriously. Many families have begun to repent in the five areas, and we are seeing God do some amazing things. One of the amazing things that He has done is give us a church building, fully furnished, free and clear. We had been renting public school buildings, churches, and whatever we could until we could build our own building. As we began to repent God gave us a sign, showing us, "You are on the right track. Keep putting me first and return to me." If God can suddenly hand us a fully furnished church, I know that if many Christians repent, He could straighten out our economy and again give us leaders that fear His holy name. He does not need us to stand up for His name. He needs us to be holy and He will give glory to His name.

As our country continues to look to man for the healing of our economy, let's turn back to the One who actually controls all things. Let's turn back to the One who can turn all things around and make our silver and gold increase. Set aside to pay the Lord first and then figure out the rest of your bills. No matter what debts you have, the debt to the Lord should be paid first.

Some might say, "But, Dave, I only make three hundred dollars a week." If that is what God has blessed you with then thirty dollars of it is holy and it is to be brought into the church. Remember, it was the woman who gave all that she had out of her poverty that the Lord was pleased with and not the people who gave out of their wealth (Luke 21:1–4). Give to God first and then watch what He will do.

BRING IN THE TITHES AND OFFERINGS

I will not rob God. I will bring in the whole tithe and offering. I will do this cheerfully because I love and trust God for all of my blessings. I also realize that our nation is under a curse because of our unfaithfulness in this area. (2 Corinthians 8:19; 9:6–7; Malachi 3:6–18; Matthew 23:23)

FOR GOD TO HEAL OUR LAND, WE MUST TURN BACK TO HIM

Use the next page or two to write out a prayer of repentance. Ask the Lord to reveal to you any ways that you are not honoring His law. In your prayer, ask the Lord to forgive you for any of the commitments that you have been deceived by Satan. Be specific as to how you have broken God's law. Then, thank the Lord for forgiving you! Finally, ask the Lord for wisdom and strength to get rid of any moral filth and to keep these commitments. Be as specific as you can to remind yourself later what the Lord is telling you now.

PRAYER

PRAYER

LESSON FIVE
MAKE DISCIPLES

HOW IS OUR FRUIT?

> *John 15:4–16 (NLT): Remain in me, and I will remain in you. For a branch cannot produce fruit if it is severed from the vine, and you cannot be fruitful unless you remain in me. Yes, I am the vine; you are the branches. Those who remain in me, and I in them, will produce _____ (1) fruit. For apart from me you can do nothing. . . . When you produce _____ (2) fruit, you are my true disciples. . . . When you obey my commandments, you remain in my love, just as I obey my Father's commandments and remain in his love. I have told you these things so that you will be filled with my joy. Yes, your joy will overflow! . . . You didn't choose me. I chose you. I appointed you to go and produce _____ (3) fruit, so that the Father will give you whatever you ask for, using my name.*

Fruit is described figuratively throughout the Scripture. There are two main meanings in the life of a believer:

Your _____ **(4):** What type of character is the Lord producing in your life? Are you showing evidence that the fruit of the Spirit is in you? Are you showing evidence that you are being holy as He is holy? (Romans 1:13)

New _____ **(5):** People coming to Christ or growing in their relationship with Christ because of your testimony and your being faithful to Christ's command to be His witness. (Acts 1:8; 1 Corinthians 16:15)

Remember the statistic from Code Blue Rally mentioned earlier:

* 88 percent of students from "Christian" homes deny their faith before they graduate from college (http://codebluerally.com/info.php).

The statistics clearly reveal to us that our fruit is becoming rotten and it is infecting all of us, so what are we to do?

LIVE YOUR LIFE TO HEAR JESUS SAY, "WELL DONE"

> ***Matthew 25:21:*** *His master replied, "Well done, good and faithful servant! You have been _____ (6) with a few things; I will put you in charge of many things. Come and share your master's happiness!"*

When we stand before the Lord on judgment day what will He be saying "well done" for? Will He be saying, "Well done . . .

- o you watched the most _____ (7) and TV.
- o you can quote so many "famous" movie lines.
- o you were so faithful to your local sports team.
- o your children were so involved in extracurricular activities.
- o you stayed so _____ (8) building your "bigger barn."

> ***Luke 12:16–20:*** *And he told them this parable: "The ground of a certain rich man produced a good crop. He thought to himself, 'What shall I do? I have no place to store my crops.' Then he said, 'This is what I'll do. I will tear down my barns and build bigger ones, and there I will store all my grain and my goods. And I'll say to myself, "You have plenty of good things laid up for many years. Take life _____ (9); eat, drink and be merry." But God said to him, 'You fool! This very night your life will be demanded from you. Then who will get what you have prepared for yourself?'"*

WHAT ARE OUR GOALS?

As parents what do we encourage our children toward? Do we encourage them to know God and His Word? Do we encourage them to make disciples and to be separate from the world? Do we encourage them to get an education in order for them to get a "good" job so that they will be able to "take life _____ (10)"?

What good is it if our children get a good "worldly" education and a good job, yet they end up in _____ (11)?

WARNING AGAINST COMPLACENCY

> *Amos 6:1–7:* Woe to you who are complacent in Zion, and to you who feel secure on Mount Samaria. . . .You put off the evil day and bring near a reign of terror. You lie on beds inlaid with ivory and lounge on your _____ (12). You dine on choice lambs and fattened calves. You strum away on your harps like David and improvise on musical instruments. You drink wine by the bowlful and use the finest lotions, but you do not grieve over the ruin of Joseph. Therefore you will be among the first to go into exile; your feasting and lounging will end.

We long to be like the arrogant. We long to be wealthy, rich, and comfortable. We love to eat out and to be served, but do we long to be the _____ (13)?

To make a disciple, I must first be a _____ - (14).

ARE THERE SIGNS OF GROWTH IN YOUR LIFE?

If you have been a Christian for many years and there is no evidence that you are _____ (15) like Christ today than when you first got saved, why not?

We would rather make sure that we are _____ (16)

and comfortable than to be like Paul who said, "He beat his body and made it his slave." Do you long to be a disciple for Jesus, one who is being made holy?

JESUS' TEACHINGS

Matthew 28:19–20: Therefore go and _____ (17) disciples of all nations, baptizing them in the name of the Father and of the Son and of the Holy Spirit, and teaching them to obey _____ (18) I have commanded you.

Mark 8:34–35: Then he called the crowd to him along with his disciples and said: "If anyone would come after me, he must deny himself and take up his cross and follow me. For whoever wants to save his life will lose it, but whoever loses his life for me and for the _____ (19) will save it."

Matthew 7:13–14: Enter through the narrow gate. For wide is the gate and broad is the road that leads to destruction, and many enter through it. But small is the gate and narrow the road that leads to life, and only a _____ (20) find it.

The Great Commission is for every believer and not just for the pastor. Where are you going? What are you teaching? What Scriptures are you sharing with others? In what ways have you laid your life down for Jesus and the gospel?

THE WIDE ROAD THAT LEADS TO DESTRUCTION

Satan, the minister of some light, leads people down the wide road of destruction. Can you see the deceptions and the twisted truths?

NEW TESTAMENT TEACHINGS ON DISCIPLESHIP

Ephesians 4:20–24: *You, however, did not come to know Christ that way. Surely you heard of him and were taught in him in accordance with the truth that is in Jesus. You were taught, with regard to your former way of life, to _____ _____ (21) your old self, which is being corrupted by its deceitful desires; to be made new in the attitude of your minds; and to put on the new self, created to be like God in true righteousness and holiness.*

Ephesians 5:3–7: *But among you there must not be even a _____ (22) of sexual immorality, or of any kind of impurity, or of greed, because these are improper for God's holy people. Nor should there be obscenity, foolish talk or coarse joking, which are out of place, but rather thanksgiving. For of this you can be sure: No immoral, impure or greedy person—such a man is an idolater—has any inheritance in the kingdom of Christ and of God. Let no one deceive you with empty words, for because of such things God's wrath comes on those who are disobedient. Therefore do not be _____ (23) with them.*

Are we being partners with the disobedient when we buy their movies, music, books, and whatever else that the disobedient present to us?

THE 5 COMMITMENTS OF DISCIPLESHIP

We must first _____ (24) and apply them to our lives and grow in our relationship with Christ. Then we can teach others what it means to know Christ.

1. *Abstain from immorality*
   (Curse for following the world)

2. *Make prayer and God's Word a priority*
   (Curse for forgetting God's law)

3. *Honor the Sabbath*
   (Curse for desecrating the Sabbath)

4. *Bring in the tithes and offerings*
   (Curse for robbing God)

5. *Make disciples*
   (Curse for disobedience and the next generation suffers)

GO AND MAKE

I have been blessed by God to see many people accept Christ as their Lord and Savior. I have never had anyone just come up to me without any prior conversation and say, "How can I be saved?" I have had to make a _____ (25) to go to them.

> *2 Timothy 1:7:* For God did not give us a spirit of timidity, but a spirit of power, of love and of self-discipline.

MAKE THE DECISION TO GO

What about you? What about your family? Who is on your prayer list that your family is reaching out to? Perhaps if we stopped chasing after

the things of this world, we would see the many lost
_____ (26) in our country.

LOOK AT THE PEOPLE AROUND YOU

Make a list of the people you know who do not know Christ or are no longer going to church. Have your children make a list of the people in their lives as well. Begin to pray for them. Begin to pray Scriptures over them. Ask the Lord to reveal to you ways that you can be reaching out to them.

> ***Luke 16:9:*** *I tell you, use _____ (27) wealth to gain friends for yourselves, so that when it is gone, you will be welcomed into eternal dwellings.*

> ***1 Peter 4:9 (NLT):*** *_____ (28) share your home with those who need a meal or a place to stay.*

> ***Hebrews 13:2 (NLT):*** *Don't forget to show hospitality to strangers, for some who have done this have entertained angels without realizing it!*

Be obedient and God will bless you tremendously and you will see much fruit.

LOOK AT THE PEOPLE AROUND YOUR CHURCH

> ***2 Corinthians 5:17–20:*** *Therefore, if anyone is in Christ, he is a new creation; the old has gone, the new has come! All this is from God, who reconciled us to himself through Christ and gave us the _____ (29) of reconciliation: that God was reconciling the world to himself in Christ, not counting men's sins against them. And he has committed to us the message of reconciliation. We are therefore Christ's ambassadors, as though God were making his appeal through us. We implore you on Christ's behalf: Be reconciled to God.*

A few years ago a member in our church felt led by God to get a degree in sign language. Then, just this year, our deaf neighbor came and knocked on our door wanting to come to a Bible study. A few weeks later she accepted Christ and has been attending church ever since.

What will God do in your life and the life of your church? What will He do for our country if we will repent?

NAMES TO BEGIN PRAYING ABOUT

_____

_____

_____

_____

SCRIPTURES TO BEGIN PRAYING

> *Acts 26:18:* To _____ (30) their eyes and turn them from darkness to light, and from the power of Satan to God, so that they may receive forgiveness of sins and a place among those who are sanctified by faith in me.

Pray that their eyes would be opened to the gospel.

> *Colossians 4:2–4:* Devote yourselves to prayer, being watchful and thankful. And pray for us, too, that God may _____ ____ _____ (31) for our message, so that we may proclaim the mystery of Christ, for which I am in chains. Pray that I may proclaim it clearly, as I should.

Pray that God would give you boldness, an opportunity, and clarity as you share the message.

IDEAS FOR REACHING OUT TO PEOPLE

Have them over; invite them to church; do something fun like bowling, playing miniature golf, or going for dessert. Live your life with the purpose of hearing Jesus say to you, "Well done, my good and faithful servant." Write down some of your own ideas to reach out to others. Plan with your family what you will do.

_____

_____

_____

_____

MAKE DISCIPLES

I will be a disciple maker. I realize the moral decay of the church and our country, and I am willing to call people back to God. I understand that I will be persecuted, but I am willing to stand up for Jesus and make disciples. (Mark 8:34, 35; Matthew 5:10; 28:18–20; John 15:4–16; Luke 16:9; 2 Timothy 1:7; 3:12; Galatians 2:20; 1 John 2:6; Amos 6:1–7; Ezekiel 3:18–20; Acts 20:26; 26:18; 2 Corinthians 5:17–20)

BEFORE THE FINAL LESSON READ THROUGH:

COMMITMENT FIVE   *107*

REFLECTION   *123*

DEDICATION   *133*

COMMITMENT 5
MAKE DISCIPLES

THE FIFTH COMMITMENT:

MAKE DISCIPLES

I will be a disciple maker. I realize the moral decay of the church and our country, and I am willing to call people back to God. I understand that I will be persecuted, but I am willing to stand up for Jesus and make disciples. (Mark 8:34, 35; Matthew 5:10; 28:18–20; John 15:4–16; Luke 16:9; 2 Timothy 1:7; 3:12; Galatians 2:20; 1 John 2:6; Amos 6:1–7; Ezekiel 3:18–20; Acts 20:26; 26:18; 2 Corinthians 5:17–20)

HOW IS OUR FRUIT?

> *John 15:4–16 (NLT):* *Remain in me, and I will remain in you. For a branch cannot produce fruit if it is severed from the vine, and you cannot be fruitful unless you remain in me. Yes, I am the vine; you are the branches. Those who remain in me, and I in them, will produce much fruit. For apart from me you can do nothing. . . . When you produce much fruit, you are my true disciples. . . . When you obey my commandments, you remain in my love, just as I obey my Father's commandments and remain in his love. I have told you these things so that you will be filled with my joy. Yes, your joy will overflow! . . . You didn't choose me. I chose you. I appointed you to go and produce lasting fruit, so that the Father will give you whatever you ask for, using my name.*

Fruit is described figuratively throughout the Scripture. There are two main meanings in the life of a believer:

Your Character: What type of character is the Lord producing in your life? Are you showing evidence that the fruit of the Spirit is in you? Are you showing evidence that you are being holy as He is holy? (Romans 1:13)

New Believers: People coming to Christ or growing in their relationship with Christ because of your testimony and your being faithful to Christ's command to be His witness. (Acts 1:8; 1

Corinthians 16:15)

George Barna divides the generations into different categories as to when an individual was born. He describes them as Builders (1927–1945), Boomers (1946–1964), Busters (1965–1983), and Mosaics (1984–2002).

He presents in many of his books and on his Web site the moral decay of our society. Each generation is moving farther from God. The builders are stronger in their faith and more consistent in their spiritual disciplines. They are more committed to their church attendance, quiet times, and their beliefs about the authority of God's Word (www.barna.org).

Remember the statistic from Code Blue Rally mentioned earlier:

* 88 percent of students from "Christian" homes deny their faith before they graduate from college (http://codebluerally.com/info.php).

The statistics clearly reveal to us that our fruit is becoming rotten and it is infecting all of us, so what are we to do? What are we doing wrong in our discipleship process? Jesus clearly told us that we are to produce much fruit and that if we will remain in Him, it will happen. We will see it by the Spirit of God living through us in the evidence of our ability to be Christlike. We will see the character of God and the fruit of the Spirit in our lives. We will see the transformation of people being born again and freed from sin. We will see our children becoming missionaries, preachers, and evangelists no matter what profession God places them in. Perhaps our focus is off when we see that 88 percent of our children are leaving the faith. We have already presented four very clear areas where many Christians today are not following God's way and we are reaping the consequences of our sin. Let's refocus.

LIVE YOUR LIFE TO HEAR JESUS SAY, "WELL DONE"

Matthew 25:21: His master replied, "Well done, good and faithful servant! You have been faithful with a few things; I will put you in charge of many things. Come and share your master's happiness!"

When we stand before the Lord on judgment day what will He be saying "well done" for? Will He be saying, "Well done . . .

- o you watched the most movies and TV.
- o you can quote so many "famous" movie lines.
- o you were so faithful to your local sports team.
- o your children were so involved in extracurricular activities.
- o you stayed so busy building your "bigger barn."

Luke 12:16–20: And he told them this parable: "The ground of a certain rich man produced a good crop. He thought to himself, 'What shall I do? I have no place to store my crops.' Then he said, 'This is what I'll do. I will tear down my barns and build bigger ones, and there I will store all my grain and my goods. And I'll say to myself, "You have plenty of good things laid up for many years. Take life easy; eat, drink and be merry." But God said to him, 'You fool! This very night your life will be demanded from you. Then who will get what you have prepared for yourself?'"

WHAT ARE OUR GOALS?

As parents what do we encourage our children toward? Do we encourage them to know God and His Word? Do we encourage them to make disciples and to be separate from the world? Do we encourage them to get an education in order for them to get a "good" job so that they will be able to "take life easy"? What is the most honorable profession? Is it doctor, lawyer, CEO, or manager? What about pastor or missionary? Do you encourage your children to get an education and to study to make good grades but find that you do not encourage them to memorize Scripture and to read their Bibles? What about teaching them to have a quiet time and to hear the voice of God? What about teaching them to seek the face of God for the path that He has called them to? What if God called your child to be a missionary? Would you support that calling or would you encourage your child to get a good job here in order for them to take life easy. Is it in this life that we are to be taking life easy, or is it in the life to come? Are we confused about the fact that this is our time of testing to see if we will be true disciples? What good is it if our children get a good "worldly" education and a good job, yet they end up in hell? Have we been so desensitized by the movies that we believe that good people go to heaven?

When we repeatedly watch movies that do not depict the regenerating process of Christ's salvation in our life, we lose our zeal for witnessing and we become convinced that good people go to heaven. This belief slowly draws us away from the truth. We begin to sympathize with the characters. We so want them to be "saved" that we push the truth to the back of our minds and we begin to believe the lie. If you do not believe the lie, then why are you not telling others how to be saved? Why have you not knocked on your neighbors' door or asked your co-worker to attend church with you? Why have you not given anyone a gospel tract in a long time? Why do we allow our own children to go off to a school that we know encourages partying and we justify it and say that at least they are getting an education? Will the education save them? Will any of their good works save them? No, they must repent and be born again.

WARNING AGAINST COMPLACENCY

> **Amos 6:1–7:** Woe to you who are complacent in Zion, and to you who feel secure on Mount Samaria. . . .You put off the evil day and bring near a reign of terror. You lie on beds inlaid with ivory and lounge on your couches. You dine on choice lambs and fattened calves. You strum away on your harps like David and improvise on musical instruments. You drink wine by the bowlful

and use the finest lotions, but you do not grieve over the ruin of Joseph. Therefore you will be among the first to go into exile; your feasting and lounging will end.

We long to be like the arrogant. We long to be wealthy, rich, and comfortable. We love to eat out and to be served, but do we long to be the servant? In our churches today it is hard to find volunteers to serve in the life of the body. Why? Because we do not want to do anything for free. We want to get paid. We want to be served or to get something for our efforts. What about doing it for the glory of God? Many growing churches all across our country are finding out that if they want to have a good program, they need to hire people to do it. If they do not hire them, they will not serve faithfully. Shouldn't we long to come and fulfill our purposes in the body and not long to be served? Yes, some need to be paid, but it is getting out of hand. Do you serve in church? Do you teach your children to serve in church? How many Christians go from one church to another trying to get their needs met? They are not looking for a place to serve. What is your part in the body? Is it to sit and be fed or is it to serve in some capacity? Many Christian parents just want to drop their kids off at Sunday school and they think that Sunday school will replace their responsibility to train their children in God's Word at home. Scripture, morals, and values must be taught at home and then reinforced at church. Remember the verses from Deuteronomy when it says talk about the Scriptures when we sit at home. All day long we are to be teaching our children the Scriptures and how to live a holy life pleasing to the Lord. Men, you will be held more accountable in this area than your wives. You are the head of the home and the duty falls upon you. Even if you are not the main teacher, you are to be making sure that discipleship is going on in your home.

To make a disciple, I must first be a disciple.

ARE THERE SIGNS OF GROWTH IN YOUR LIFE?

If you have been a Christian for many years and there is no evidence that you are more like Christ today than when you first got saved, why not? The call to be a follower of Christ is that we follow Him and obey, His teachings. The more we follow and obey the more we become like Him. We should be growing in our Scripture knowledge, our prayers, our ability to witness and share, pray in public, and our ability to forgive. We should also be growing in the fruit of the Spirit. Our love, joy, peace, patience, kindness, goodness, faithfulness, gentleness, and self-control should be maturing in us.

Do you have a besetting sin that is the same this year as it was last year? Part of God's filling in us is the self-control to defeat our flesh. We are to be putting to death our sinful nature by the power of the Holy Spirit in us. Christ has already paid for that sin, and people should see the progression of our Christlikeness in front of them. Non Christians know that they are powerless over sin and they want to see the answer to their struggles. Jesus is the answer and we are to work out our salvation with fear and trembling. Let's cling to Jesus and let Him heal and free us in order for the world to see His power. Remember that it is by grace that we are able to "say 'No' to ungodliness and worldly passions, and to live self-controlled, upright and godly lives in this present age" (Titus 2:12). The reason we do not see the power is because we are chasing after the things of this world and we are not chasing after Jesus. We would rather live in our sin and make sure that we are entertained and comfortable than to be like Paul who said, "He beat his body and made it his slave." Do you long to be a disciple for Jesus, one who is being made holy?

"I could never pray out loud or speak in front of a group," you might say. Guess what? I took speech class in the summer because I was terrified of speaking in front of others. Today, by God's grace, I speak weekly in front of a congregation. Moses felt the same way, and others have felt the uneasiness that many feel when they are asked by God to be His witness. Just because we feel scared to share with others does not mean that God is not asking us to make disciples. We are to seek Him for the words, power, and ability to fulfill His calling in us. You may never be a teacher in front of a large congregation, but I'm sure that you could be a huge influence to the people around you. You could be inviting them to come to a Bible study that you are a part of and sharing how you are applying God's Word to your everyday life. You do not have to be the main teacher, but you need to be a part of the discipleship process. Let God live through you and you will be amazed at what He does in and through you. Be willing. Be available. Be listening.

JESUS' TEACHINGS

> *Matthew 28:19–20:* *Therefore go and make disciples of all nations, baptizing them in the name of the Father and of the Son and of the Holy Spirit, and teaching them to obey everything I have commanded you.*

When was the last time that you taught your children or your friend something about the Scriptures? We are to be teaching them to obey everything that Jesus commanded us. Do we do this? Do we do this when we sit down to watch a movie and immorality shows up? What do we do? Do you turn it off and say, "As Christians we do not support things that take the Lord's name in vain. Deuteronomy 5:11 says, 'You shall not misuse the name of the LORD your God, for the LORD will not hold anyone guiltless who misuses his name.' Children, it is important for us to come out from the world and be separate." Do we look at Second John and talk about how we do not want to share in the wicked work of the world? It is my prayer that this book and workbook will be a tool that will help us get back to discipleship. We need to be calling our children and our generation back to God. If we do not, we will lose even more of our freedoms.

> *Mark 8:34–35:* *Then he called the crowd to him along with his disciples and said: "If anyone would come after me, he must deny himself and take up his cross and follow me. For whoever*

wants to save his life will lose it, but whoever loses his life for me and for the gospel will save it."

Deny our self from what? From the fleshly things that war against our soul. Our flesh longs to be served and to be first, but in Christ we learn how to serve and to think of others better than ourselves. We learn that even if we enjoy it, that does not make it right.

> **Matthew 7:13–14:** *Enter through the narrow gate. For wide is the gate and broad is the road that leads to destruction, and many enter through it. But small is the gate and narrow the road that leads to life, and only a few find it.*

The world is pulling us onto the wide path, and it is the path of destruction. The world is leading us and we are being the tail. We must repent and once again be the head. We must set the example in righteousness based upon God's Word. We must get the cursing, the taking of the Lord's name in vain, and the sexual immorality out of our homes and lives. We must get back on the narrow road and call them to follow us. If we will touch no unclean thing God will receive us. He is holy and He cannot be around even one sin.

The Great Commission is for every believer and not just for the pastor. How are you going? Where are you going? What are you teaching? What Scriptures are you sharing with others? In what ways have you laid your life down for Jesus and the gospel? How are you setting the example to walk down the narrow road?

THE WIDE ROAD THAT LEADS TO DESTRUCTION

Satan, the minister of some light, leads people down the wide road of destruction. Can you see the deceptions and the twisted truths?

NEW TESTAMENT TEACHINGS ON DISCIPLESHIP

> **Ephesians 4:20–24:** *You, however, did not come to know*

Christ that way. Surely you heard of him and were taught in him in accordance with the truth that is in Jesus. You were taught, with regard to your former way of life, to put off your old self, which is being corrupted by its deceitful desires; to be made new in the attitude of your minds; and to put on the new self, created to be like God in true righteousness and holiness.

What deceitful desires are you putting off (abstaining from)?

> ***Ephesians 5:3–7:*** *But among you there must not be even a hint of sexual immorality, or of any kind of impurity, or of greed, because these are improper for God's holy people. Nor should there be obscenity, foolish talk or coarse joking, which are out of place, but rather thanksgiving. For of this you can be sure: No immoral, impure or greedy person—such a man is an idolater—has any inheritance in the kingdom of Christ and of God. Let no one deceive you with empty words, for because of such things God's wrath comes on those who are disobedient. Therefore do not be partners with them.*

Are we being partners with the disobedient when we buy their movies, music, books, and whatever else that the disobedient present to us? What other Scriptures warn us about being in the world but not of it? Are there hints of sexual immoralities in our lives? I am so surprised at how many people call themselves Christians and they are living with someone of the opposite sex. Some Christians even come to their defense and they say, "But maybe they are not doing anything immoral." The fact that they are giving a hint of immorality is immoral. As Ephesians chapter five verse three tells us, there must not be even a hint of sexual immorality or of any kind of impurity. We have become so desensitized to what holiness is that many no longer see things clearly. Do we have hints of immorality in our movie and music collections or anything else that we own? Some of us do not have hints but we have blatant immoralities in our homes.

THE 5 COMMITMENTS OF DISCIPLESHIP

As we begin to recommit our lives to Jesus to be holy as He is holy, we can use the five commitments as a tool of repentance and discipleship. We must first repent and apply them to our lives and grow in our relationship with Christ. Then we can teach others what it means to know Christ.

1. *Abstain from immorality*
   (Curse for following the world)

2. *Make prayer and God's Word a priority*
   (Curse for forgetting God's law)

3. *Honor the Sabbath*
   (Curse for desecrating the Sabbath)

4. *Bring in the tithes and offerings*
   (Curse for robbing God)

5. *Make disciples*
   (Curse for disobedience and the next generation suffers)

GO AND MAKE

I have been blessed by God to see many people accept Christ as their Lord and Savior. I have never had anyone just come up to me without any prior conversation and say, "How can I be saved?" I have had to make a decision to go to them. I have had to make a decision to pray for and share with them. I have had to prepare myself with knowing the gospel in order to share the gospel. Are you preparing yourself to be a spokesman for God who is not ashamed? They will not come to us— we are to go to them. We are to pray for them. We are to bring up the conversation and direct it toward spiritual things. Some of the best training tools to witness are *The Way of the Master* by Ray Comfort and

117

Kirk Cameron and *Share Jesus Without Fear* by William Fay.

> **2 Timothy 1:7:** *For God did not give us a spirit of timidity, but a spirit of power, of love and of self-discipline.*

MAKE THE DECISION TO GO

Pick up your cross and head toward the ministry that God has given you. My wife, Christy, and I pray and ask the Lord to reveal to us whom we are to be reaching out to for salvation and discipleship. Through our AWANA program we met a family that wasn't attending church regularly. We began to pray for them and then invite them over for dinner. We began to build a relationship with them, and through this we have seen the dad come to Christ. He is an alcoholic that has been set free by Jesus. His family is now coming to Church as well. It took us getting out of our comfort zone and inviting them over for dinner. It took prayer. It took the Spirit of God directing our steps. Have we pursued others that have not accepted the message? Yes, but that doesn't mean we stop. We keep going and we keep reaching to seek and to save the lost as Jesus has taught us. What about you? What about your family? Who is on your prayer list that your family is reaching out to? Even your young children can be praying and sharing Christ. Every believer needs to make the decision to go and to seek after people that God has placed around you. Whom are you to be reaching out to? Your neighbor, co-worker, family member? Perhaps if you invited them over for dinner, they might just come to church with you or hear what you have to say as to how Jesus has changed your life. Perhaps if we stopped chasing after the things of this world, we would see the many lost souls in our country.

LOOK AT THE PEOPLE AROUND YOU

Make a list of the people you know who do not know Christ or are no longer going to church. Have your children make a list of the people in their lives as well. Begin to pray for them. Begin to pray Scriptures over them. Ask the Lord to reveal to you ways that you can be reaching out to them.

> *Luke 16:9:* I tell you, use worldly wealth to gain friends for yourselves, so that when it is gone, you will be welcomed into eternal dwellings.

With all of the money that you will be saving from not participating in the world you can now invest in kingdom things. Invite people over to dinner or take them out for dessert. Buy them a Bible or a good Christian book. Just go and have a cup of coffee with them and share with them what the Lord is doing in your life.

> *1 Peter 4:9 (NLT):* Cheerfully share your home with those who need a meal or a place to stay.

> *Hebrews 13:2 (NLT):* Don't forget to show hospitality to strangers, for some who have done this have entertained angels without realizing it!

Be careful as you choose your disciples that you do not show favoritism. God may be calling you to the down and out, the prisoners, the widows, or orphans. We have followed the world so long that we want to have friends that look and act a certain way, but your ministry may be in the nursing home. Be obedient and God will bless you tremendously and you will see much fruit.

LOOK AT THE PEOPLE AROUND YOUR CHURCH

> *2 Corinthians 5:17–20:* Therefore, if anyone is in Christ, he is a new creation; the old has gone, the new has come! All this is from God, who reconciled us to himself through Christ and gave us the ministry of reconciliation: that God was reconciling the world to himself in Christ, not counting men's sins against them. And he has committed to us the message of reconciliation. We are therefore Christ's ambassadors, as though God were making his appeal through us. We implore you on Christ's

behalf: Be reconciled to God.

Our church began to reevaluate our ministries. One area that we changed was our Sunday school. We canceled it and put our efforts into a ministry called the Good News Club based out of Child Evangelism Fellowship. We did not feel that we could do both and so we focused our efforts on the GNC. This is a program to teach the gospel in the public school system. We went from about 10 church kids to 69 kids enrolled with many being unchurched. We are seeing God move in powerful ways. I am not telling any church to get rid of their Sunday school programs, but I am telling them to seek God and ask Him if you could make your program better or if you should be going in a different direction.

Since we have begun to work on the five commitments, we are seeing God do some awesome things in our lives and the lives of our church. People with drug addictions are being set free. A few years ago a member in our church felt led by God to get a degree in sign language. Then, just this year, our deaf neighbor came and knocked on our door wanting to come to a Bible study. A few weeks later she accepted Christ and has been attending church ever since.

I have been witnessing for many years, but I can tell you that since we have made this decision to repent, we have seen more power in our witnessing efforts. I am doing less arm twisting and saying, "Wow God, that was awesome!" People are being drawn to our church. We have visitors almost every week and I wonder how they are finding us. For instance, I mentioned before that we rent a church building on Sunday nights. One night before our evening service a man called and, since kids will be kids, some of them kept hanging up on him. He persistently kept calling. Finally, an adult answered the phone and the young man in his twenties said that he would like to come to our church if he could get a ride. A member went and picked him up. After the service he told me that this is the church for him. He has been studying the Word, and he feels that the church needs to get more serious about their relationship with Christ. When asked how he found us, he just said that he "looked in the phone book and felt lead to call that number."

I preached this message at a church in Sedalia, Missouri, and they are seeing God do some awesome things as well. They are repenting in these five areas and God is blessing them. They are seeing people that they have been witnessing to for years show up on Sunday. They had a deaf family call the church and say that they feel like they need to get serious about their relationship with God. They are seeing God heal and restore broken relationships, and this is only the beginning. What will God do in your life and the life of your church? What will He do for our country if we will repent?

NAMES TO BEGIN PRAYING ABOUT

_____

_____

_____

_____

SCRIPTURES TO BEGIN PRAYING

Acts 26:18: To open their eyes and turn them from darkness to light, and from the power of Satan to God, so that they may receive forgiveness of sins and a place among those who are sanctified by faith in me.

Pray that their eyes would be opened to the gospel.

Colossians 4:2–4: Devote yourselves to prayer, being watchful and thankful. And pray for us, too, that God may open a door for our message, so that we may proclaim the mystery of Christ, for which I am in chains. Pray that I may proclaim it clearly, as I should.

Pray that God would give you boldness, an opportunity, and clarity as you share the message.

IDEAS FOR REACHING OUT TO PEOPLE

Have them over; invite them to church; do something fun like bowling, playing miniature golf, or going for dessert. Live your life with the purpose of hearing Jesus say to you, "Well done, my good and faithful servant." Write down some of your own ideas to reach out to others. Plan with your family what you will do.

_____

_____

_____

_____

MAKE DISCIPLES

I will be a disciple maker. I realize the moral decay of the church and our country, and I am willing to call people back to God. I understand that I will be persecuted, but I am willing to stand up for Jesus and make disciples. (Mark 8:34, 35; Matthew 5:10; 28:18–20; John 15:4–16; Luke 16:9; 2 Timothy 1:7; 3:12; Galatians 2:20; 1 John 2:6; Amos 6:1–7; Ezekiel 3:18–20; Acts 20:26; 26:18; 2 Corinthians 5:17–20)

REFLECTION

Have you ever been to youth camp or another type of religious camp and afterward you felt so close to God? Why did you feel closer to God at the end of camp and gradually lose that fire? At camp you were constantly digging into the Word and filling yourself with God through your Bible studies and your worship experiences and the godly people around you that helped to fan your spiritual flame. When you left camp, you had to make a decision as to what you would continue to fill your life with. Unfortunately, this youth camp cycle is similar to the bigger cycle that our nation is in. We have decided not to live everyday as if we were at youth camp, and we have decided to follow the ways of this empty world. Many youth camps ask the kids not to bring their secular music, they have no televisions to fill their minds with the desires of the world, and they constantly encourage them to grow in their relationship with God. Shouldn't this be our goal every day? Are we not commanded to come out from the world and to live separate lives that are filled with the same youth-camp joy all year long? The televisions, radios, mp3 players, and whatever else brings instruction are not evil in themselves. It is what we are allowing them to play that make them evil. Sanctify your life and all that you can control. Keep your lives free from the evil desires of the flesh, and watch how you can have your youth-camp experience all year long. Be filled with the Spirit of God!

During these cycles in the Old Testament what do you think the nation of Israel was thinking right before they went into slavery? Were they thinking, "We really need to repent in order for God to begin to restore our land"? Or were they thinking, "We are not being too bad. Surely God will take care of us. After all, we are His people." We sometimes feel the same way and we add to their statements that we "prayed a prayer." If they could see the destruction coming, why didn't they turn from their ways? Can we see the destruction coming? Are we ready to turn from our wicked ways?

We have been on a journey that has revealed to us specific ways that we need to change. Some may need only to improve in one area; others may need to improve in all five areas. The important thing is that we repent. The battle is not in knowing what is right. The battle begins when your flesh tells you not to obey. Repentance is not easy. Changing old habits is not easy, but it is necessary in our country. Live by the power of the Holy Spirit and you will not gratify the desires of your flesh.

In Second Chronicles chapter seven Solomon and the nation are dedicating the temple, and the Lord presents to them a reaffirmation of the principles of His blessings and curses. He reminds them that He will bless them and provide for them as long as they will follow His ways, but He says . . .

> **2 Chronicles 7:19–22:** *But if you turn away and forsake the decrees and commands I have given you and go off to serve other gods and worship them, then I will uproot Israel from my land, which I have given them, and will reject this temple I have consecrated for my Name. I will make it a byword and an object of ridicule among all peoples. And though this temple is now so imposing, all who pass by will be appalled and say, "Why has the LORD done such a thing to this land and to this temple?" People will answer, "Because they have forsaken the LORD, the God of their fathers, who brought them out of Egypt, and have embraced other gods, worshiping and serving them—that is why he brought all this disaster on them."*

The temple is no longer there. Why? Because the nation went off and served other gods and followed the ways of the people around them. We are doing the same thing. Can we see how important it is for us to stop living our way and to start following the ways of Christ? The teaching of sanctification and holiness is leaving the church and we are making the gospel into a license for immorality—something that Jude and other New Testament authors warned us against. We are to become holy as He is holy. That is our calling. That is what the Lord is longing to do in and through us. The issue becomes, Are we acting, speaking, and loving like Christ? To be in an intimate relationship with Christ, we must come out from the world and touch no unclean thing.

In Galatians the apostle Paul teaches us about this sanctification process.

> **Galatians 5:16–17:** *So I say, live by the Spirit, and you will not gratify the desires of the sinful nature. For the sinful nature desires what is contrary to the Spirit, and the Spirit what is contrary to the sinful nature. They are in conflict with each other, so that you do not do what you want.*

I love how the NIV puts it, "so that you do not do what you want." We have a flesh and it desires to go the way of the world, but we are called to follow the ways of Christ. Look what Paul says in this verse.

> **Galatians 2:20–21:** *I have been crucified with Christ and I no longer live, but Christ lives in me. The life I live in the body, I live by faith in the Son of God, who loved me and gave himself for me. I do not set aside the grace of God, for if righteousness could be gained through the law, Christ died for nothing!*

We must crucify our desires that go against the ways of God. Just because we long to go see a certain movie does not make it right. Just because we do not want to bring in the tithe does not make it right. Just because we do not want to pray and read our Bibles does not make it right. Just because we are shy and do not want to share with others does not make it right. What makes it right or wrong is if Jesus would be doing it. Would Jesus be bringing in His tithe and offerings? Yes. Would Jesus be going to this movie that takes His name in vain? No. Would Jesus be seeking to save the lost? Yes. Would Jesus be praying, memorizing, and reading God's Word? Yes. Then the conclusion is that we are called to do the same. He is the standard against which we will be judged.

In verse twenty-one Paul says that he does not "set aside the grace of God, for if righteousness could be gained through the law, Christ died for nothing!" It is because Christ died and freed us from our sin and He empowers us to holy living. It is Christ in us that helps us turn away from evil and live a self-controlled, upright, and godly life in this present age. We are called to such a life.

> **Romans 8:29:** *For those God foreknew he also predestined to be conformed to the likeness of his Son, that he might be the firstborn among many brothers.*

We are called to be conformed unto the likeness of Christ.

> **Romans 2:13:** *For it is not those who hear the law who are righteous in God's sight, but it is those who obey the law who will be declared righteous.*

It is not those who attend church and hear about the gospel, but it is those that become like Christ who will be declared righteous. Would Jesus be abstaining from immorality? Would Jesus be praying and reading the Word? Would Jesus be honoring the Sabbath? Would Jesus be bringing in the tithes and offerings? Would Jesus be making disciples? If so, then we are to walk as He would walk.

> **Romans 8:3–4:** *For what the law was powerless to do in that it was weakened by the sinful nature, God did by sending his own Son in the likeness of sinful man to be a sin offering. And so he condemned sin in sinful man, in order that the righteous requirements of the law might be fully met in us, who do not live according to the sinful nature but according to the Spirit.*

Sin has been condemned in us. We are to be putting it to death in our lives and becoming more holy in order for the righteous requirements of the law to be fully met in us. To Jesus be the glory for what He is and what He will do in our lives!

THE 5 COMMITMENTS

Let's review the 5 commitments and evaluate our response.

The First Commitment: Abstain from Immorality—I commit that I will abstain from whatever presents immorality as acceptable. I will be aware of Satan's tricks and I will stand up for God's morals. I will get rid of the moral filth, based upon God's Word, that I have allowed into my life and I will be holy to the Lord. (Deuteronomy 7:26; 8:10–14; 1 John 5:19; Ephesians 2:2; 5:3–7; 2 John 2:7–11; James 1:21; Exodus 20:7; Colossians 3:8; 1 Peter 2:11; 1 John 1:8, 9)

What will you do in abstaining from immorality? Will you continue to own, rent, and go see movies that have immoralities in them? Will you continue to support and share in the wicked work of the world? Will you continue to read magazines, books, and other material that Jesus would never endorse or own? Will you continue to listen and own music that promotes immorality? Will you stop doing want you want to do and start allowing the Holy Spirit to empower you to righteousness?

Remember that God is holy and He cannot be around even one sin. Just one curse word, taking of the Lord's name in vain, or even a hint of immorality makes it unholy.

Will you repent as the nations before you and get rid of the moral filth that you have acquired? Will you sanctify your home and all that you own? If you own a business, then sanctify it; if you play music at your business, then sanctify that music. Do not worry about the world; trust in God and live to glorify His name. Will you be persecuted? Yes. Will people in the church persecute you? Yes. Did they persecute Jesus? Yes.

> *Matthew 5:11–12:* *Blessed are you when people insult you, persecute you and falsely say all kinds of evil against you because of me. Rejoice and be glad, because great is your reward in heaven, for in the same way they persecuted the prophets who were before you.*

Don't keep putting it off. Repent for our country and the generations to come. Repent, for the Lord's return may be near and He is not coming back for a dirty and stained bride. He is coming back for a pure and spotless bride!

Write out a prayer or a commitment on this topic. Be specific with what the Lord is telling you to do.

The Second Commitment: Make Prayer and God's Word a Priority—I will make prayer and God's Word a priority in my life and my family's life. I will discipline myself to my quiet times and I will make opportunities where we read and pray together as a couple or family. (Matthew 4:4; Psalm 1:1; 119:11; Deuteronomy 6:4–9; 32:45–47; I Thessalonians 5:17; Hebrews 4:12)

Will you get the dust off your Bible and begin to read His Word? Pray for wisdom and understanding. Seek His face. Remember that without His Holy Spirit and power in your life you will always eat the tempting apple. The problem with temptation is that it is so tempting. Our flesh desires evil. We must fill ourselves with the Spirit of God and that is done by His Word, praise, and prayer. If we try to do it on our own, we will justify our actions and blind ourselves as the nations before us who went into slavery. We need to repent and beg God to heal our land.

Will you get your family on the right track again? Will you make time to read and pray together?

Write out a prayer or a commitment on this topic. Be specific with what the Lord is telling you to do.

The Third Commitment: Honor the Sabbath—I commit that I will no longer miss church for work, for things of this world, for entertainment, for laziness, or for selfish reasons. I will no longer honor the changing of the blue law, but I will honor God's Law. I realize that I reap what I sow. I am ready to stand up for Jesus and His Word and to call the church back to Him. (Isaiah 56:2; 58:13,14; 1 John 2:15–17; James 4:4; Leviticus 19:1–3; Exodus 20: 8–11; 31:13–17; Acts 20:7; Revelation 1:10)

Will you stop desecrating the Sabbath? Will you stop eating out and shopping on the Sabbath? Will you stop causing your man and maidservant to work? Will you stop missing church for selfish reasons and realize that it has consequences?

Write out a prayer or a commitment on this topic. Be specific with what the Lord is telling you to do.

The Fourth Commitment: Bring in the Tithes and Offerings—I will not rob God. I will bring in the whole tithe and offerings. I will do this cheerfully because I love and trust God for all of my blessings. I also realize that our nation is under a curse because of our unfaithfulness in this area. (2 Corinthians 8:19; 9:6–7; Malachi 3:6–18; Matthew 23:23)

Will you trust God with your finances and bring in the tithe? Will you listen to His voice and obey when He asks you for an offering? Will you stop robbing God and saying that it is futile to serve the Lord?

Write out a prayer or a commitment on this topic. Be specific with what the Lord is telling you to do.

The Fifth Commitment: Make Disciples—I will be a disciple maker. I realize the moral decay of the church and our country and I am willing to call people back to God. I understand that I will be persecuted, but I am willing to stand up for Jesus and make disciples. (Mark 8:34, 35; Matthew 5:10; 28:18–20; John 15:4–16; Luke 16:9; 2 Timothy 1:7; 3:12; Galatians 2:20; 1 John 2:6; Amos 6:1–7; Ezekiel 3:18–20; Acts 20:26; 26:18; 2 Corinthians 5:17–20)

Will you stop the pursuit of wealth and riches and begin to pursue Jesus and building His kingdom? Will you take the time to study God's Word in order for you to teach others? Will you listen to the voice of God and begin reaching out to the people He has placed around you? Will you pray for them? Will you teach your children how to pray for and make disciples? Will you realize that discipleship does not stop at their confession of Christ?

Write out a prayer or a commitment on this topic. Be specific with what the Lord is telling you to do.

DEDICATION

In each of the five commitments we are looking at God's standards and calling people to live and act like Him. This chapter is a call to you as an individual and as a church to spur one another on.

YOU ARE NOT GIVING UP; YOU ARE GAINING BLESSINGS

In one way repentance is hard and it is self-denial, but on the other hand it is awesome and it means blessings. The only thing you are really giving up is the empty way of life handed down to us by the generation before us. Think about it. How many people are confused, depressed, lonely, unfulfilled, complainers, unable to sleep, addicted, angry, bitter, and even suicidal? Why are they this way?

> *I Peter 1:18: For you know that it was not with perishable things such as silver or gold that you were redeemed from the empty way of life handed down to you from your forefathers.*

We have been redeemed from this empty unfulfilling life, and we have been given life to its fullness.

> *John 10:10: The thief comes only to steal and kill and destroy; I have come that they may have life, and have it to the full.*

This full life is in obediently following Jesus. We are His followers and we are laying our lives down to build His Kingdom for His glory. In this we have life in all its fullness. We do not get a fulfilled life by getting a great education, having a lot of money, or chasing after the ways and things of this world. Wherever He leads, we should go. In fact, if we choose to be a friend of the world, we become an enemy of God and we suffer the consequences.

James 4:4: You adulterous people, don't you know that friendship with the world is hatred toward God? Anyone who chooses to be a friend of the world becomes an enemy of God.

† Let's stop running to the theater every time they say jump.
† Let's stop supporting immoralities presented as acceptable.
† Let's turn off the prime-time shows that have immoralities in them.
† Let's listen and read only things that build us up in the faith.
† Let's recommit ourselves to our quiet times and family devotional times.
† Let's stop shopping and eating out on the Sabbath.
† Let's stop trying to build our kingdom in order for us to take life easy.
† Let's awaken to the lost souls around us and begin to pray for and reach out to them that they would be saved.
† Let's be holy as He is holy.

DEDICATION

To dedicate: to devote to the worship of a divine being; specifically: to set apart to sacred uses with solemn rites (We are the temple of the Holy Spirit); to commit to a goal or way of life (To be holy)

> *I Peter 1:14–16: As obedient children, do not conform to the evil desires you had when you lived in ignorance. But just as he who called you is holy, so be holy in all you do; for it is written: "Be holy, because I am holy."*

As the Lord has opened my eyes, my prayer is that your eyes have been opened as well. What will you do now? Will you begin to ask the Holy Spirit for help in order for you to abstain from the ways of this world, or will you continue to go along with the crowd, even the crowd in church? We need mighty men and women of God who will humbly call the church back to God. Will you call others to the five commitments? Will you consecrate yourself to be holy?

We have the option: we can continue to watch and own things that go against His Word; we can continue to desecrate the Sabbath by working and shopping; we can continue to ignore our quiet times and the responsibility of teaching our children His Word; we can continue to allow the generations behind us to suffer. Or we can repent.

Repentance is hard. It takes self-denial and abstaining from our fleshly desires, but it is the call of God on our lives. We are to become like Jesus in everything we do.

It is time for us to stand up and tell the world that we are going to live according to God's law and accept His ways as our standard of living. We were created by God, and God is our Lord, and His standards will be our standards. We will be holy to the Lord. We will no longer follow the ways of the world.

OBEDIENCE EQUALS BLESSINGS

What will the Lord do in and through your life? What will the Lord do in and through your church?

CONSECRATE YOURSELVES

> *Leviticus 11:44:* I am the LORD your God; consecrate yourselves and be holy, because I am holy.

We have already spoken about how the Lord wants us to be sanctified. He longs to mold us to be more and more like Himself, holy.

> *Ephesians 1:4:* For he chose us in him before the creation of the world to be holy and blameless in his sight.

We are not only told that we are to be holy, but we are to be for God a kingdom of priests and a holy nation (1 Corinthians 1:2; Hebrews 12:4; 1 Peter 1:15, 16).

> *1 Peter 2:9:* But you are a chosen people, a royal priesthood, a holy nation, a people belonging to God, that you may declare the praises of him who called you out of darkness into his wonderful light.

In the Old Testament the priests had to take great care in how they acted and what they wore. They lived their lives as an instrument for the Lord's purposes. They took great care in putting on all of the garments just as the Lord required. One of the last pieces that the priests had to put on was a gold plate that was engraved. They would tie this plate with a blue cord and attach it to their turban that was worn on their head. This plate would be across their forehead and it read, "Holy to the Lord."

> *Exodus 39:27–31* For Aaron and his sons, they made tunics of fine linen—the work of a weaver—and the turban of fine linen, the linen headbands and the undergarments of finely twisted linen. The sash was of finely twisted linen and blue, purple and scarlet yarn—the work of an embroiderer—as the LORD commanded Moses. They made the plate, the sacred diadem, out of pure gold and engraved on it, like an inscription on a seal: HOLY TO THE LORD. Then they fastened a blue cord to it to attach it to the turban, as the LORD commanded Moses.

> *Deuteronomy 7:6:* For you are a people holy to the LORD your God.

At our church, we have purchased many gold plates and asked the people to wear them across their foreheads. No, we didn't do that, but we did purchase many wristbands that said, "Holy to the Lord." After we had gone through a study of the five commitments, we had a dedication ceremony and asked the people to repent and consecrate themselves to the Lord. We presented to them exactly what you have gone through in this book, and we challenged them to commit to the five commitments.

At the end of our ceremony we encouraged them to come forward and take a wristband to wear as a symbol of their repentance and a reminder to them of the commitment that they have made.

The wristband, of course, has no power, but it is a good reminder to live their life as if Jesus was living through them—to make every decision of their life as Jesus would; to watch, listen, and read only what He would; to discipline themselves to their quiet times and to lead others to do the same; to no longer desecrate the Sabbath; to bring in their tithes and offerings; and to call others to repentance and commit to building the Lord's Kingdom.

LET THE GLORY OF THE LORD FILL YOUR TEMPLE

When Solomon had finished building the temple for the Lord, he prayed a prayer of dedication. In his prayer he spoke of the cycle that we go through and what we need to do when we turn away from God and bring destruction upon ourselves.

> *2 Chronicles 6:36–41: When they sin against you—for there is no one who does not sin—and you become angry with them and give them over to the enemy, who takes them captive to a land far away or near; and if they have a change of heart in the land where they are held captive, and repent and plead with you in the land of their captivity and say, "We have sinned, we have done wrong and acted wickedly"; and if they turn back to you with all their heart and soul in the land of their captivity where they were taken, and pray toward the land you gave their fathers, toward the city you have chosen and toward the temple I have built for your Name; then from heaven, your dwelling place, hear their prayer and their pleas, and uphold their cause. And forgive your people, who have sinned against you.*
>
> *"Now, my God, may your eyes be open and your ears attentive to the prayers offered in this place.*

"Now arise, O LORD God, and come to your resting place, you and the ark of your might. May your priests, O LORD God, be clothed with salvation, may your saints rejoice in your goodness.

We need to pray and ask the Lord to forgive us of our sins. We need to have a change of heart before we go further into captivity. Before the Lord would bless the temple with His presence, the people would have to prepare the temple exactly as He commanded. It had to be done according to His standards and not their own. For God to fill the temple, they had to purify everything and make preparations for His glory to dwell. As the New Testament says,

> **1 Corinthians 3:16:** *Don't you know that you yourselves are God's temple and that God's Spirit lives in you?*

We are the temple of the living God and we need to make preparations for His glory to dwell in us in power. The Bible also tells us to be filled with the Holy Spirit and to not grieve the Spirit. Sin grieves the Spirit and it separates us from the glory of God. God cannot be around sin and we should desire His presence in our lives and not love things of this world. We are to guard our hearts and turn our eyes and ears away from worthless things. If we will prepare ourselves and turn away from our evil ways, then the glory of the Lord will again fill our temples and His hands of protection will lead and guide us. We may have to endure the end times, but we can do this in His power as the apostles did before us. Once we have repented . . .

> **2 Chronicles 7:1–3:** *When Solomon finished praying, fire came down from heaven and consumed the burnt offering and the sacrifices, and the glory of the LORD filled the temple. The priests could not enter the temple of the LORD because the glory of the LORD filled it. When all the Israelites saw the fire coming down and the glory of the LORD above the temple, they knelt on the pavement with their faces to the ground, and they worshiped and gave thanks to the LORD, saying, "He is good; his love endures forever."*

THE LORD WILL BE OUR BANNER

I am proud to be an American and I like our flag that declares freedom. I also realize that the freedoms and the prosperity that we have enjoyed have been given to us by God. As proud as I am to be an American, there is another banner that I want to see again in our country. I want to see the banner of the Lord over us. I want to see His glory again protecting us and driving out the evil in front of us.

When the nation of Israel was led out of Egypt the Lord led them by a cloud by day and a fire at night.

> *Exodus 13:21: By day the LORD went ahead of them in a pillar of cloud to guide them on their way and by night in a pillar of fire to give them light, so that they could travel by day or night.*

Can you imagine what other nations saw when they looked upon the nation of Israel? They saw a pillar of fire that was over them at night. They saw a nation go off into the desert and then come out bigger and stronger than ever. The Lord kept their shoes and clothes from wearing out, and He fed them when there was nothing else around to eat or drink. The Lord knows how to protect His obedient children, and that is the banner that I want over us—the banner of His love and protection.

> *Exodus 14:24–25: During the last watch of the night the LORD looked down from the pillar of fire and cloud at the Egyptian army and threw it into confusion. He made the wheels of their chariots come off so that they had difficulty driving. And the Egyptians said, "Let's get away from the Israelites! The LORD is fighting for them against Egypt."*

The Lord can heal our land and drive out our enemies if we will repent and return to Him as our first love. This cry is similar to the call that we have examples of throughout Scripture. When the nation began to realize that they were wandering away from the ways of the Lord, a proclamation would be made. Elijah said it this way:

> *I Kings 18:21:* Elijah went before the people and said, "How long will you waver between two opinions? If the LORD is God, follow him; but if Baal is God, follow him."

Joshua said it this way:

> *Joshua 24:14–15:* "Now fear the LORD and serve him with all faithfulness. Throw away the gods your forefathers worshiped beyond the River and in Egypt, and serve the LORD. But if serving the LORD seems undesirable to you, then choose for yourselves this day whom you will serve, whether the gods your forefathers served beyond the River, or the gods of the Amorites, in whose land you are living. But as for me and my household, we will serve the LORD."

OUR "MEMORIAL STONE"—THE WRISTBAND

> *I Samuel 7:12:* Then Samuel took a stone and set it up between Mizpah and Shen. He named it Ebenezer, saying, "Thus far has the LORD helped us."

> *I Peter 1:13–16:* Therefore, prepare your minds for action; be self-controlled; set your hope fully on the grace to be given you when Jesus Christ is revealed. As obedient children, do not conform to the evil desires you had when you lived in ignorance. But just as he who called you is holy, so be holy in all you do; for it is written: "Be holy, because I am holy."

> *I Peter 2:9–12:* But you are a chosen people, a royal priesthood, a holy nation, a people belonging to God, that you may declare the praises of him who called you out of darkness into his wonderful light. Once you were not a people, but now you are the people of God; once you had not received mercy, but now you have received mercy. Dear friends, I urge you, as

aliens and strangers in the world, to abstain from sinful desires, which war against your soul. Live such good lives among the pagans that, though they accuse you of doing wrong, they may see your good deeds and glorify God on the day he visits us.

OUR DEDICATION

I will dedicate myself to the five commitments of repentance. I symbolize my commitment by coming forward and taking a wristband to wear. In my coming, I am asking the Lord to forgive me and asking the church to hold me accountable to these commitments. (If you would like to purchase wristbands, you can go to our Web site)

The prayer of our church is for our country to repent and get back to the blessings of God. We are on the verge of going into slavery, and we need to turn from our wicked ways and ask the Lord to heal our land. The Lord's return may be soon and we need to be preparing our wedding garments for the ceremony.

Check out our Web site, www.fivecommitments.com, and encourage others to repent. Encourage your church to be a five-commitment church. Let's begin to shock the world and have them wonder what is going on with the Christians. Why do they no longer support our movies, music, and books? Why do they no longer support businesses on Sunday? How are they prospering so much in this recession?

If you have repented and God is blessing you for your obedience, we want to post your story of encouragement on our Web site.

May the Lord forgive us and heal our land.

Run to win the prize,

David Lange

DANIEL'S PRAYER

Daniel 9:4–19: I prayed to the LORD my God and confessed: "O Lord, the great and awesome God, who keeps his covenant of love with all who love him and obey his commands, we have sinned and done wrong. We have been wicked and have rebelled; we have turned away from your commands and laws. We have not listened to your servants the prophets, who spoke in your name to our kings, our princes and our fathers, and to all the people of the land.

"Lord, you are righteous, but this day we are covered with shame—the men of Judah and people of Jerusalem and all Israel, both near and far, in all the countries where you have scattered us because of our unfaithfulness to you. O LORD, we and our kings, our princes and our fathers are covered with shame because we have sinned against you. The Lord our God is merciful and forgiving, even though we have rebelled against him; we have not obeyed the LORD our God or kept the laws he gave us through his servants the prophets. All Israel has transgressed your law and turned away, refusing to obey you.

"Therefore the curses and sworn judgments written in the Law of Moses, the servant of God, have been poured out on us, because we have sinned against you. You have fulfilled the words spoken against us and against our rulers by bringing upon us great disaster. Under the whole heaven nothing has ever been done like what has been done to Jerusalem. Just as it is written in the Law of Moses, all this disaster has come upon us, yet we have not sought the favor of the LORD our God by turning from our sins and giving attention to your truth. The LORD did not hesitate to bring the disaster upon us, for the LORD our God is righteous in everything he does; yet we have not obeyed him.

"Now, O Lord our God, who brought your people out of Egypt with a mighty hand and who made for yourself a name that endures to this day, we have sinned, we have done wrong. O Lord, in keeping with all your righteous acts, turn away your anger and your wrath from Jerusalem, your city, your holy hill. Our sins and the iniquities of our fathers have made Jerusalem and your people an object of scorn to all those around us.

"Now, our God, hear the prayers and petitions of your servant. For your sake, O Lord, look with favor on your desolate sanctuary. Give ear, O God, and hear; open your eyes and see the desolation of the city that bears your Name. We do not make requests of you because we are righteous, but because of your great mercy. O Lord, listen! O Lord, forgive! O Lord, hear and act! For your sake, O my God, do not delay, because your city and your people bear your Name."

LESSON SIX
DEDICATION

In each of the five commitments we are looking at God's
_____ (1) and calling people to live and act like Him.

YOU ARE NOT GIVING UP; YOU ARE GAINING BLESSINGS

In one way repentance is hard and it is self-denial, but on the other hand it is awesome and it means blessings.

> *I Peter 1:18: For you know that it was not with perishable things such as silver or gold that you were redeemed from the _____ (2) way of life handed down to you from your forefathers.*

> *John 10:10: The thief comes only to steal and kill and destroy; I have come that they may have life, and have it to the _____ (3)*

This full life is in obediently _____ (4) Jesus.

> *James 4:4: You adulterous people, don't you know that friendship with the world is hatred toward God? Anyone who chooses to be a friend of the world becomes an _____ (5) of God.*

  † Let's stop running to the theater every time they say jump.
  † Let's stop supporting immoralities presented as
    _____ (6).
  † Let's turn off the prime-time shows that have immoralities in them.
  † Let's listen and read only things that build us up in the faith.

† Let's _____ (7) ourselves to our quiet times and family devotional times.
† Let's stop shopping and eating out on the Sabbath.
† Let's stop trying to build our kingdom in order for us to take life easy.
† Let's awaken to the lost souls around us and begin to pray for and reach out to them that they would be saved.
† Let's be _____ (8) as He is holy.

DEDICATION

To dedicate: to devote to the worship of a divine being; specifically: to set apart to sacred uses with solemn rites (We are the _____ (9) of the Holy Spirit); to commit to a goal or way of life (To be holy)

> *I Peter 1:14–16:* As obedient children, do not conform to the evil desires you had when you lived in ignorance. But just as he who called you is holy, so be holy in _____ (10) you do; for it is written: "Be holy, because I am holy."

We need mighty men and women of God who will humbly call the church back to God. Will you call others to the five commitments? Will you consecrate yourself to be holy?

We have the option: we can continue to watch and own things that go against His Word; we can continue to desecrate the Sabbath by working and shopping; we can continue to ignore our quiet times and the responsibility of teaching our children His Word; we can continue to allow the generations behind us to suffer. Or we can _____ (11).

OBEDIENCE EQUALS BLESSINGS

What will the Lord do in and through your life? What will the Lord do in and through your church?

CONSECRATE YOURSELVES

Leviticus 11:44: I am the LORD your God; _____ (12) yourselves and be holy, because I am holy.

Ephesians 1:4: For he chose us in him before the creation of the world to be holy and blameless in his sight.

1 Peter 2:9: But you are a chosen people, a royal priesthood, a holy nation, a people belonging to God, that you may declare the praises of him who called you out of darkness into his wonderful light.

In the Old Testament the priests had to take great care in how they acted and what they wore.

Exodus 39:27–31 For Aaron and his sons, they made tunics of fine linen—the work of a weaver—and the turban of fine linen, the linen headbands and the undergarments of finely twisted linen. The sash was of finely twisted linen and blue, purple and scarlet yarn—the work of an embroiderer—as the LORD commanded Moses. They made the plate, the sacred diadem, out of pure gold and engraved on it, like an inscription on a seal: _____ (13) TO THE LORD. Then they fastened a blue cord to it to attach it to the turban, as the LORD commanded Moses.

Deuteronomy 7:6: For you are a people holy to the LORD your God.

At the end of our ceremony we want to encourage you to take a wristband to wear as a symbol of your repentance and a reminder to you of the commitment you will make.

LET THE GLORY OF THE LORD FILL YOUR TEMPLE

When Solomon had finished building the temple for the Lord, he prayed a prayer of dedication. In his prayer he spoke of the cycle that we go through and what we need to do when we turn away from God and bring destruction upon ourselves.

> *2 Chronicles 6:36–41: When they sin against you—for there is no one who does not sin—and you become angry with them and give them over to the enemy, who takes them captive to a land far away or near; and if they have a change of heart in the land where they are held captive, and repent and plead with you in the land of their captivity and say, "We have sinned, we have done wrong and acted _____ (14)"; and if they turn back to you with all their heart and soul in the land of their captivity where they were taken, and pray toward the land you gave their fathers, toward the city you have chosen and toward the temple I have built for your Name; then from heaven, your dwelling place, hear their prayer and their pleas, and uphold their cause. And forgive your people, who have sinned against you.*
>
> *"Now, my God, may your eyes be open and your ears attentive to the prayers offered in this place.*
>
> *"Now arise, O LORD God, and come to your resting place, you and the ark of your might. May your priests, O LORD God, be clothed with salvation, may your saints rejoice in your goodness.*
>
> *1 Corinthians 3:16: Don't you know that you yourselves are God's temple and that God's Spirit _____ (15) in you?*

We are the temple of the living God and we need to make preparations for His glory to dwell in us in power. Once we have repented . . .

2 Chronicles 7:1–3: *When Solomon finished praying, fire came down from heaven and consumed the burnt offering and the sacrifices, and the glory of the LORD _____ (16) the temple. The priests could not enter the temple of the LORD because the glory of the LORD filled it. When all the Israelites saw the fire coming down and the glory of the LORD above the temple, they knelt on the pavement with their faces to the ground, and they worshiped and gave thanks to the LORD, saying, "He is good; his love endures forever."*

THE LORD WILL BE OUR BANNER

I want to see the banner of the Lord over us. I want to see His glory again protecting us and driving out the evil in front of us.

When the nation of Israel was led out of Egypt the Lord led them by a cloud by day and a fire at night.

Exodus 13:21: *By day the LORD went ahead of them in a pillar of cloud to guide them on their way and by night in a _____ (17) of fire to give them light, so that they could travel by day or night.*

The Lord knows how to protect His obedient children, and that is the banner that I want over us—the banner of His love and protection.

Exodus 14:24–25: *During the last watch of the night the LORD looked down from the pillar of fire and cloud at the Egyptian army and threw it into confusion. He made the wheels of their chariots come off so that they had difficulty driving. And the Egyptians said, "Let's get away from the Israelites! The _____ (18) is fighting for them against Egypt."*

The Lord can heal our land and drive out our enemies if we will repent and return to Him as our first love. This cry is similar to the call that we have examples of throughout Scripture. When the nation began to realize that they were wandering away from the ways of the Lord, a proclamation would be made. Elijah said it this way:

> **1 Kings 18:21:** *Elijah went before the people and said, "How long will you waver between two opinions? If the LORD is God, _____ (19) him; but if Baal is God, follow him."*

Joshua said it this way:

> **Joshua 24:14–15:** *"Now fear the LORD and serve him with all faithfulness. _____ _____ (20) the gods your forefathers worshiped beyond the River and in Egypt, and serve the LORD. But if serving the LORD seems undesirable to you, then choose for yourselves this day whom you will serve, whether the gods your forefathers served beyond the River, or the gods of the Amorites, in whose land you are living. But as for me and my household, we will _____ (21) the LORD."*

OUR "MEMORIAL STONE"—THE WRISTBAND

> **1 Samuel 7:12:** *Then Samuel took a stone and set it up between Mizpah and Shen. He named it Ebenezer, saying, "Thus far has the LORD helped us."*

> **1 Peter 1:13–16:** *Therefore, prepare your minds for action; be self-controlled; set your hope fully on the grace to be given you when Jesus Christ is revealed. As obedient children, do not _____ (22) to the evil desires you had when you lived in ignorance. But just as he who called you is holy, so be holy in all you do; for it is written: "Be holy, because I am holy."*

> **1 Peter 2:9–12:** *But you are a chosen people, a royal priesthood, a holy nation, a people belonging to God, that you may declare the praises of him who called you out of darkness*

into his wonderful light. Once you were not a people, but now you are the people of God; once you had not received mercy, but now you have received mercy. Dear friends, I urge you, as aliens and strangers in the world, to _____ (23) from sinful desires, which war against your soul. Live such good lives among the pagans that, though they accuse you of doing wrong, they may see your good deeds and glorify God on the day he visits us.

OUR DEDICATION

I will dedicate myself to the five commitments of repentance. I symbolize my commitment by coming forward and taking a wristband to wear. In my coming, I am asking the Lord to forgive me and asking the church to hold me accountable to these commitments.

Let's begin to shock the world and have them wonder what is going on with the Christians. Why do they no longer support our movies, music, and books? Why do they no longer support businesses on Sunday? How are they prospering so much in this recession?

May the Lord forgive us and heal our land.

The Lord's return may be soon and we need to be preparing our wedding garments for the ceremony.

SNARES OF SATAN

Below is a list of some of the immoralities our world is presenting to us as acceptable. Next to the immorality is a reference to God's view on the topic.

WE ABSTAIN FROM WHATEVER PRESENTS IMMORALITY AS ACCEPTABLE.

Imagine placing a chocolate cake in front of a three-year-old and saying to that child, "Now, do not eat this cake." What if you placed a freshly baked cake in front of the child day after day? Eventually that child is going to succumb to fleshly desires and indulge in that delicious temptation. It is the same with us. Our flesh desires sin and sin is gratifying for the moment, but there are consequences to our disobedience.

Satan does not put chocolate cake in front of us, but he presents fleshly desires in front of us daily through so many avenues. There are temptations all around us, and they are increasing because Christians are no longer saying no to immoralities. We are accepting them into our lives and homes. When we accept them over and over into our lives through our media choices, eventually we are going to act upon our sinful desires. As the statistics reveal, the young people in the church of our generation are acting out the immoralities that we are allowing them to be presented with daily.

There are so many shows, songs, magazines, and books that are presenting to us that casual sex is moral. The Bible calls this sexual immorality, but the longer we allow our children to watch, listen, and read about these temptations, the more likely it is that they are going to eventually eat the cake. Many Christian children are not only eating the cake but they are leaving the church confused and deceived about the truth. As Christian parents we need to be sitting down with our children and teaching them how to abstain from immoralities and what

God's Word says. Not only are we not to commit the sin, but we are told not to associate with those that act in such ways. When we allow music, movies, magazines, and whatever other influences there may be into our lives, we are accepting them and bringing destruction into our homes.

Use this "Snares of Satan" guide to get God's perspective on the issues of our day.

Abortion How is Satan trying to get our culture to accept this as normal or moral? What avenues is he using to get us to accept this?

What do these verses tell us about God's view on this topic? (Exodus 20:13; Psalm 139:13–16; Acts 17:26, 27)

Anger / Rage / Violence How is Satan trying to get our culture to accept this as normal or moral? What avenues is he using to get us to accept this?

What do these verses tell us about God's view on this topic? (Ephesians 4:31; Colossians 3:8; Matthew 5:21–22; 1 Peter 3:9–12)

Being Drunk / Drugs How is Satan trying to get our culture to accept this as normal or moral? What avenues is he using to get us to accept this?

What do these verses tell us about God's view on this topic? (Romans 13:13; 1 Thessalonians 5:7, 8; 1 Corinthians 6:9, 10; Ephesians 5:18; 1 Peter 4:7)

Cohabitation / Living Together How is Satan trying to get our culture to accept this as normal or moral? What avenues is he using to get us to accept this?

What do these verses tell us about God's view on this topic? (Hebrews 13:4; 1 Peter 2:12; Ephesians 5:3)

Disrespecting or Disobeying Authority How is Satan trying to get our culture to accept this as normal or moral? What avenues is he using to get us to accept this? Have you noticed the cartoons of our day and how disrespectful some are?

What do these verses tell us about God's view on this topic? (Leviticus 19:32; 1 Peter 2:17; Exodus 20:12; Romans 13:1–3)

Divorce How is Satan trying to get our culture to accept this as normal or moral? What avenues is he using to get us to accept this?

What do these verses tell us about God's view on this topic? (Malachi 2:15, 16; Mark 10:2–9; Matthew 5:31, 32; 1 Corinthians 7:10–15)

Focusing on Outward Beauty How is Satan trying to get our culture to accept this as normal or moral? What avenues is he using to get us to accept this?

What do these verses tell us about God's view on this topic? (1 Samuel 16:7; 1 Peter 3:3, 4; 1 Timothy 2:9, 10)

Gluttony How is Satan trying to get our culture to accept this as normal or moral? What avenues is he using to get us to accept this?

What do these verses tell us about God's view on this topic? (Proverbs 23:1–3, 20, 21; 28:7; 1 Corinthians 6:12, 13; 19–20; 10:31)

Greed / Gambling How is Satan trying to get our culture to accept this as normal or moral? What avenues is he using to get us to accept this?

What do these verses tell us about God's view on this topic? (Colossians 3:5; Luke 12:15–21; 1 Timothy 6:6–10; Hebrews 13:5; Proverbs 23:4; 28:20; Ephesians 5:3, 7)

Homosexuality How is Satan trying to get our culture to accept this as normal or moral? What avenues is he using to get us to accept this?

What do these verses tell us about God's view on this topic? (Leviticus 18:22; Romans 1:26, 27, 32; 1 Corinthians 6:9–11)

Lack of Commitment to Church How is Satan trying to get our culture to accept this as normal or moral? What avenues is he using to get us to accept this?

What do these verses tell us about God's view on this topic? (Hebrews 10:25; Ephesians 3:10; 4:16)

Lack of Commitment to Prayer and Bible Reading How is Satan trying to get our culture to accept this as normal or moral? What avenues is he using to get us to accept this?

What do these verses tell us about God's view on this topic? (Deuteronomy 6:4–9; 32:45–47; Matthew 4:4; 1 Thessalonians 5:17; 1 Peter 4:7; Jude 1:20; Psalms 1:2; 119:11; 2 Timothy 3:14–17)

Not Making Disciples How is Satan trying to get our culture to accept this as normal or moral? What avenues is he using to get us to accept this?

What do these verses tell us about God's view on this topic? (Matthew 4:19; 28:18–20 John 14:12, 23, 24; 20:21; Mark 6:12; Acts 1:8; 4:31; 8:4; 2 Corinthians 5:17; 6:2)

Pornography / Nudity / Lust How is Satan trying to get our culture to accept this as normal or moral? What avenues is he using to get us to accept this?

What do these verses tell us about God's view on this topic? (Job 31:1; Genesis 3:7; Colossians 3:5; Habakkuk 2:15; Matthew 5:27, 28; Galatians 5:19–21)

Profanity / Swearing How is Satan trying to get our culture to accept this as normal or moral? What avenues is he using to get us to accept this?

What do these verses tell us about God's view on this topic? (Matthew 5:33–37; 12:33–37; Colossians 3:8; 1 Peter 4:11; Ephesians 4:29)

Sexual Immorality How is Satan trying to get our culture to accept this as normal or moral? What avenues is he using to get us to accept this?

What do these verses tell us about God's view on this topic? (Song of Songs 2:7; 3:5; 8:4; 1 Thessalonians 4:3–8; Galatians 5:19; 1 Corinthians 6:12–20; Ephesians 5:3; Hebrews 13:4)

Witchcraft / Sorcery How is Satan trying to get our culture to accept this as normal or moral? What avenues is he using to get us to accept this?

What do these verses tell us about God's view on this topic? (Leviticus 19:31; 20:6; Deuteronomy 18:9–13; Galatians 5:19–21)

After you have read God's view on these topics do you see any ways in which you need to repent? Are you allowing immoralities presented as acceptable into your life and the life of your family? Are you putting the temptations right in front of them or are you scripturally teaching them the truth?

> *I John 1:5–10:* *This is the message we have heard from him and declare to you: God is light; in him there is no darkness at all. If we claim to have fellowship with him yet walk in the darkness, we lie and do not live by the truth. But if we walk in the light, as he is in the light, we have fellowship with one another, and the blood of Jesus, his Son, purifies us from all sin. If we claim to be without sin, we deceive ourselves and the truth is not in us. If we confess our sins, he is faithful and just and will forgive us our sins and purify us from all unrighteousness. If we*

claim we have not sinned, we make him out to be a liar and his word has no place in our lives.

Walk in the light with Jesus! His blessings of peace, contentment, and joy far outweigh the fleeting delights of sin that bring guilt, consequences, and pain.

If you have been ensnared by Satan and you have fallen to your fleshly desires, don't give up. Repent, so that times of refreshing may come from the Lord. Confess your sin and ask Him for the strength to turn away from it. Get involved with a Bible-believing church that will support you in your decision to follow Christ.

FOR PASTORS AND TEACHERS

My prayer and vision for this book and the workbook is for them to be used as a tool for repentance and discipleship.

The workbook is designed for you to teach through each of the five commitments. All of the material in the book is included in the workbook with teaching lessons added. After each of the teaching lessons there is reading material for students to do on their own. The last lesson is the dedication, in which you will have an opportunity to encourage students to commit to the five commitments. It is suggested that they symbolize their commitment by taking a wrist band to wear that says, "HOLY TO THE LORD." If you would like to order wristbands for your dedication check out our website.

The snares of Satan Bible study has been created for personal use, family devotions, and for small group discussions. If you know someone struggling with one of these snares read the Scriptures together to get God's perspective. Some of its subject matter is not suitable for young children.

We have created a Web site with more information.

www.fivecommitments.com

On the website:

- Free PowerPoint presentations to download that go along with the workbook.
- Bulk rates are available for you to purchase the book or the workbook.
- Wristbands—to order for your dedication service or just to use.
- We would love to hear your testimonies of how God is blessing you through your obedience in repentance.

LESSON ONE

1 God
2 *carefully*
3 *ridicule*
4 *proud*
5 wealth giver
6 *enticed*
7 *obey*
8 *curse*
9 Prayer
10 abortion
11 blue
12 *their*
13 Christian
14 **self-denial**
15 family
16 homosexuality
17 believing
18 running
19 Zero!
20 *control*
21 **desires**
22 support
23 *war*
24 *Flee*
25 TEMPLE
26 *shares*
27 SHARING
28 *all*
29 holy
30 *Testing*

31 **robots**
32 Holy Spirit
33 *righteousness*
34 *godly*
35 *requirements*
36 *unclean*
37 *abstain*
38 *conflict*
39 *must*

ANSWERS TO FILL IN THE BLANKS

LESSON TWO

1. *Impress*
2. *God-breathed*
3. *hidden*
4. *life*
5. *word*
6. *living*
7. commit
8. prayer
9. *Holy Spirit*
10. Personally
11. *Humble*
12. *Pray*
13. *Turn*
14. *got rid*
15. *rid*
16. *get rid*
17. *house*
18. *house*
19. *enemy*
20. *get rid*
21. holy
22. *want*
23. TEMPLE
24. acceptable

LESSON THREE

1. **88**
2. **alarm**
3. *holy*
4. *sign*
5. *first*
6. actions
7. selfish
8. *own*
9. *Sabbath*
10. selfish
11. Sabbath
12. Sunday
13. founded
14. any
15. *together*
16. *requirements*
17. waiters
18. wicked
19. emergency
20. milk
21. purchase
22. stressful
23. rest
24. break
25. **Bible**
26. **wrong**
27. **home**
28. *righteousness*
29. Christians

ANSWERS TO FILL IN THE BLANKS

LESSON FOUR

1. *cheerful*
2. offering
3. *they*
4. *offering*
5. tithe
6. offering
7. *tenth*
8. *tithes*
9. *offerings*
10. *curse*
11. *whole*
12. *blessed*
13. whole
14. cursing
15. *abundant*
16. *borrow*
17. *carefully*
18. *lend*
19. *prosperity*
20. *aside*
21. *holy*
22. increase
23. first

ANSWERS TO FILL IN THE BLANKS

LESSON FIVE

1. *much*
2. *much*
3. *lasting*
4. **Character**
5. **Believers**
6. *faithful*
7. movies
8. busy
9. *easy*
10. easy
11. hell
12. *couches*
13. servant
14. **disciple**
15. more
16. entertained
17. *make*
18. *everything*
19. *gospel*
20. *few*
21. *put off*
22. *hint*
23. *partners*
24. repent
25. decision
26. souls
27. *worldly*
28. *Cheerfully*
29. *ministry*
30. *open*

31. open a door

ANSWERS TO FILL IN THE BLANKS

LESSON SIX DEDICATION

1. standards
2. *empty*
3. *full.*
4. following
5. *enemy*
6. acceptable
7. recommit
8. holy
9. temple
10. *all*
11. repent
12. *consecrate*
13. *HOLY*
14. *wickedly*
15. *lives*
16. *filled*
17. *pillar*
18. *LORD*
19. *follow*
20. *Throw away*
21. *serve*
22. *conform*
23. *abstain*

NOTES

NOTES

NOTES

NOTES

NOTES